Eighteen Days in June

Robert Buelteman

Eighteen Days in June

Robert Buelteman

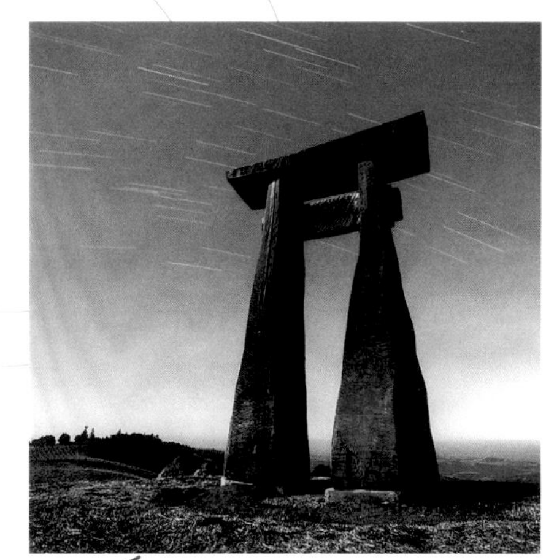

For Robert Denison

with appreciation

EIGHTEEN DAYS IN JUNE

ROBERT BUELTEMAN

Introduction
ROBERT HASS

Editor
ROBERT McDONALD

DJERASSI RESIDENT ARTISTS PROGRAM
In Association with
CUSTOM & LIMITED EDITIONS
San Francisco   New York

Published by Djerassi Resident Artists Program
2325 Bear Gulch Road
Woodside, California 94062-4405

In association with Custom & Limited Editions
41 Sutter Street #1634
San Francisco, California 94104-4903

Edited by Robert McDonald, Oakland, California
Designed by 1185 Design, Palo Alto, California

Library of Congress Cataloging-in-Publication Data

Buelteman, Robert, 1954-
    Eighteen days in June / Robert Buelteman;
introduction, Robert Hass; editor, Robert McDonald.
    p. cm.
    ISBN 1-881529-37-1
    1. Landscape photography--California--Santa Cruz
Mountains. 2. Santa Cruz Mountains (Calif.)--
Pictorial works. I. McDonald, Robert, 1933- II. Title.

TR660.5 .B84   2000
779'.3679469—dc21
                                              00-055507

Robinson Jeffers, "Pearl Harbor," *The Collected Poetry
of Robinson Jeffers*, edited by Tim Hunt, (Stanford,
California: Stanford University Press, 1991),
Volume 3, 1938-1962, pp.115-116.

Printed in Italy

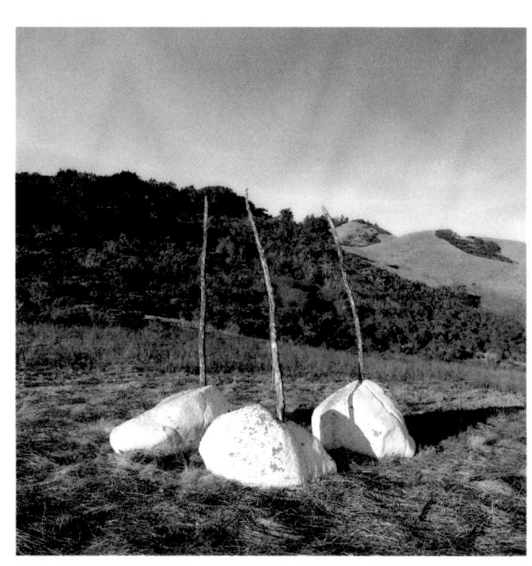

The Djerassi Resident Artists Program
and Robert Buelteman
gratefully acknowledge the donors
whose financial contributions enabled the publication of
Eighteen Days in June

Sue and John Diekman
Maxygen, Inc.

The Susie Tompkins Buell Foundation
The Star Hill Fund
Isabel Maxwell
The Overbrook Foundation
Kathleen Scutchfield
Karie Thomson

Diane Wood Middlebrook
Vibeke Strand and Jack Loftis
Dale Djerassi

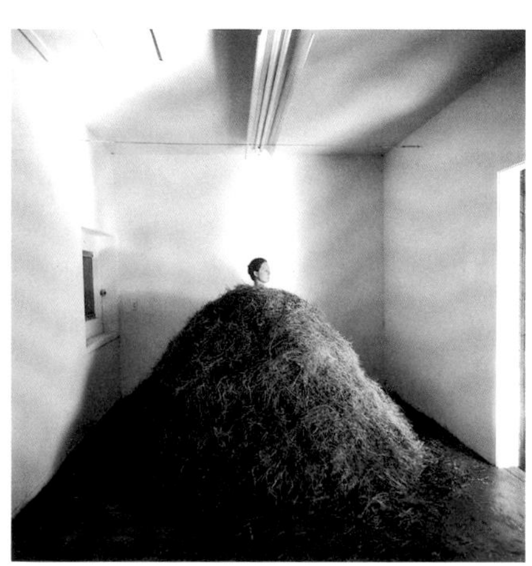

The Djerassi Resident Artists Program, for giving me "the gift of time" and for the sponsorship of my Artist's Salon in 1998.

Those who donated that rarest of gifts—their time and their personal efforts—to the Djerassi Resident Artists Program for the realization of this book:
Peggy Burke
Anne Cribbs
Sue Diekman
Dale Djerassi
Patrick Enright
Ron Fouts
Robert Hass
Robert McDonald
Diane Wood Middlebrook
Vibeke Strand

The funders of this book, who made its publication possible.

Members of my immediate family, for allowing me to be who I am—Julie, Robbie, Skyler, Bob, Betty, Anne, Jane, and Lisa.

Dennis O'Leary, Executive Director of the Djerassi Resident Artists Program, whose appreciation of my work and stewardship of this project have brought it to fulfillment.

Audrey Rust, President, Peninsula Open Space Trust, whose commission to photograph the land of the Artists Program in 1995 led to my residency and this book.

Charles Amirkhanian and Carol Law, Executive Director and General Manager, respectively, of the Djerassi Resident Artists Program in 1996, for offering me a residency.

The Peninsula Community Foundation for having funded my residency.

Dale Djerassi, whose friendship has proved resilient enough to meet the challenges of the publishing world.

Kate and Geir Jordahl, friends and artists, whose generous sharing of their years of experience and of their laboratory notes sped my inquiry into the world of the infrared, and, again, Geir Jordahl, whose beautiful book, *San Joaquin, River of Spirit*, was an inspiration for this project.

Fred Lyon, renowned photographer, longtime personal friend and mentor, for encouraging me to take risks during my residency that I would not otherwise have attempted.

Kathy Scutchfield, for supporting my work far beyond the conventional limits of friendship.

Sandra Marsh and Dan Miller, for sharing their genius with my family.

All the artists whose work I experienced during my residency, for providing me with a glimpse of the divine every day I was there, and for reminding me of the fundamental beauty of the human spirit.

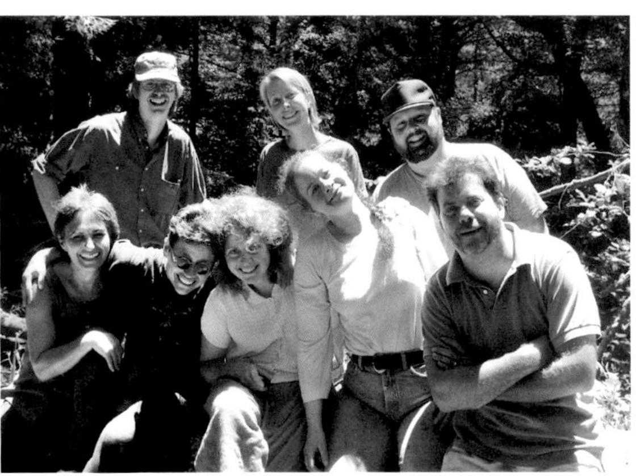

Back row, left to right: Lex Williford, Denise Newman, Wendell Mayo; *Front row, left to right:* Alisa Olmert, Gili Shanit, Susanne Cockrell, Barbara Edelstein, Robert Buelteman. *(Not Pictured:* Chryssa Udvardy, Ushio Torikai.)

In June 1996, thanks to the Djerassi Resident Artists Program, I recovered the creative vitality I had lost while coping with several family tragedies. I arrived at the ranch deep in grief and questioning the value of myself and of my work. I departed eighteen days later with a renewed love of life, a new understanding of my calling, a new body of work and a new family of friends. There at SMIP Ranch I experienced personal transformation in a setting of great natural beauty through a program created by the Djerassi family in response to its own loss and subsequent grief.

I had been unable to accept the offer of a residency in the spring because my mother, Betty, was dying of cancer. My wife's mother, Peggy, had only recently passed on due to the same disease. Then, just before arriving at the ranch, I learned that we would lose my younger sister, Lisa, to cancer as well.

I have been fortunate to have many great teachers and learning experiences in my life, but none has been greater than the awareness of my own mortality, which I acquired through the role of caregiver to my family, whom I newly saw as mortal.

The solitude and silence of the resident artist experience allowed me time for reflection not possible in the outside world. Preoccupied by day-to-day struggles to keep afloat, I easily avoided asking questions whose answers challenged my sleeping mind: Does my life have any significance to anyone but myself? If I were to pass on today, would anyone outside my family notice? Just what meaning is there to a life called to making photographs anyway?

At the Djerassi Ranch, freed of crushing distractions, I received "the gift of time" to consider these and other issues. I was there with nine other spirits whose dance of artistic expression with me over those eighteen days opened a hurt and closed heart and assisted me in my return to living.

With my artist companions, especially with Susanne Cockrell and Alisa Olmert, both of whom had also lost their mothers in recent months, I reflected on my own losses and found myself joyfully making art for the first time in eighteen months.

In the face of death I found new life with others, and for that I am deeply grateful.

—Robert Buelteman, May 2000

The mission of the Djerassi Resident Artists Program
is to support and enhance the creativity of artists
by providing uninterrupted time for work, reflection, and collegial interaction
in a setting of great natural beauty,
and to preserve the land upon which the program is situated.

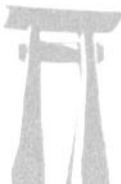

My sister, Pamela, was born in Hartford, Connecticut, on April 20, 1950. She spent her early childhood in Michigan and Mexico. When she was 10 years old we moved to California where she was educated and came of age as an artist, attending Pomona College, San Francisco Art Institute and Stanford University where she received her degree in Art.

Soon after moving to California, our family bought property in the rural, coastal mountains of San Mateo County, south of San Francisco. The land consisted of undulating grassy hills and majestic redwood forests with an expansive view of the Pacific Ocean.

There we would spend weekends hiking and playing. Eventually, we established a substantial Shorthorn cattle breeding operation on the land. We called it SMIP Ranch. SMIP—*Sic Manebimus In Pace*—'So we shall remain in peace.' My parents built a house on the ranch where they sought the solace that open space can provide. While still a student at Stanford University, I also built a house there in which my son, Alexander, and I still reside.

My sister built her house nearby, and while her husband was completing his medical school residency, she spent her days painting in her studio, riding her beloved horses over the land she cherished and tending her vegetable garden. Our lives seemed full, not least for this gift of a place for which we had developed such a deep and abiding love—a place that my sister and I called home.

On July 5, 1978, Pamela, my sole sibling and my nearest neighbor, took her life. That act, and the incalculable pain it delivered to those of us who knew and loved her, seemed to defy comprehension on any acceptable level, yet begged for some kind of meaningful response. This was the crucible from which the Djerassi Resident Artists Program was born.

Conceived by my father, Carl Djerassi, in memory of Pamela, the Djerassi Resident Artists Program was established in 1979 initially to provide a yearlong residency for one woman artist at a time to live and to work in Pamela's house and studio at SMIP Ranch.

Subsequently, with the help of my father's wife, Diane Middlebrook, the Program was expanded to include both women and men in residence together working in a variety of disciplines. The Shorthorn cattle operation had ended, allowing conversion of the main cattle barn into artists' studios and the ranch manager's house into artists' residences.

In the 1990s, the Program began the process of transformation from a private family foundation to a public charity with a board of trustees responsible for its funding and operation. Concurrent with that process, the board began discussing its responsibilities for the 600 acres of land that formed the Program's grounds.

It was my profound conviction that the preservation of the Program's land, substantially unchanged if possible, would most honor Pamela's vision of what should happen to her land.

Accordingly, I approached Audrey Rust, President of the Peninsula Open Space Trust, an organization actively dedicated to preserving land on the San Francisco Peninsula, and began the discussion that eventually led in October 1999 to the Peninsula Open Space Trust's purchase of a conservation easement that will preserve the land in perpetuity while providing valuable funds for the Program's maintenance of its land and facilities.

Robert Buelteman, who had captured the natural beauty of the area in his exquisite book, *The Unseen Peninsula,* was commissioned by the Peninsula Open Space Trust to photograph the land. These photographs prompted Charles Amirkhanian, then Executive Director of the Program, to extend the invitation of a residency to Rob. The result is the book you are holding in hand.

As I sit here on the edge of the North American continent, looking out to the Pacific Ocean, over land that is still rural with ranches and wildlife, still so similar to the view my sister held so dear, I think about the cumulative body of work created by the more than 1,000 artists who have been in residence and I find it amazing to contemplate.

This book represents the work of one such artist-in-residence. Through a serendipitous confluence of factors, it would seem that Rob was destined to make this book and that the Djerassi Resident Artists Program was destined to be its willing and grateful beneficiary.

—Dale Djerassi, April 2000

The last rays of the sun
Reach the wet earth,
Making the water sparkle
Like sequins in the dark.

The small stream spills
Down the slight slope
Creating a tiny waterfall,
Leaving behind
Small droplets to rest on the leaves,
Which then slide off
And disappear into the earth
As the sun goes down.

—Pamela Djerassi, 1966

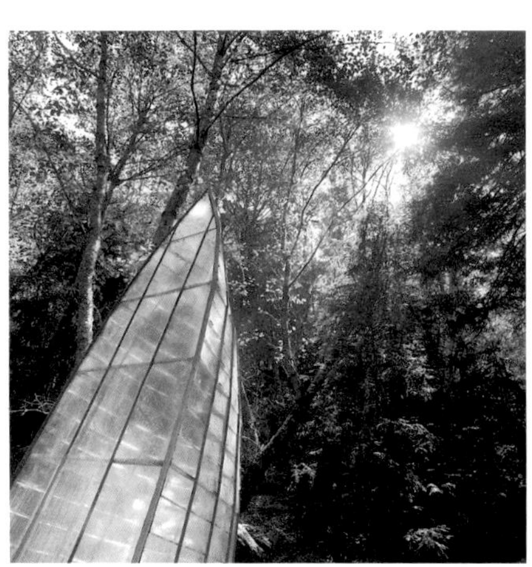

These photographs were made while Robert Buelteman was a resident in the Djerassi Resident Artists Program at Woodside, California in June of 1996. The campus of the Program, one of those dream places where artists in various disciplines are given food and lodging and a chance to work for a space of time without the world's ceaseless interruptions, is situated on six hundred acres atop the Santa Cruz Mountains above the Pacific Ocean some thirty miles south of San Francisco. So this book is, first of all, a record of what happened to one artist when he was given time and freedom and turned loose in that landscape.

And in this way it almost makes a narrative. When he came to the Djerassi Program, Buelteman had just lost his mother and his wife's mother to cancer and had received the news that his sister was dying of the same disease. The photographs are not necessarily about mourning, or grief, but the walk we are invited to take with him seems informed by those emotions. Looking at them, we come to understand that even their formal qualities are bound up with the artist's state of mind. The black border of the prints is made by clear film around the edge of the negative: it tells us that none of these images has been cropped. What Buelteman found with the camera lens is what we see. Or, rather, what we see is the composition his eye found. But the black band that frames each one belongs, beyond its technical meaning, to something like the formality of bereavement.

Another technical aspect of the photographs is the brilliances of light in them, and the thick darknesses, and the muted silvery quality of some of the backgrounds. It gives a few of the photographs, and patches of almost all of them, a strangely antique quality, as if they were tintypes, as if time in them was layered, and the images were emerging somehow from the history of photography itself. When I first looked at them, I knew enough to know that this must have something to do with the film stock, and that the final image was the work of the darkroom, and guessed that the darkroom work must have been—for the artist—one of the places where the work of discovery occurred. And part of that discovery must have been the silvery tintype greys that haunt the forest background in many of the photographs. It makes time tender.

We are so accustomed to the conventions of black and white photography that we hardly notice the fact that it is not how human beings see the world. Color photography, nearer to human sight, because it developed later and because the color in color film is so variable, never seems to us quite as real as black and white images. The association of black and white images with realism is an old one—counterintuitive, you would think, but deeply ingrained in our habits of seeing. Part of the drama of Buelteman's images is the way in which they make us reconsider that association. There is a strangeness in them, a quiet foregrounding of artifice that reminds the viewer that this is not quite how we ever see the world. The whites and grays and silvers and blacks of the medium impose their own subject, and the subject is light, what it is and what it does. You do not have to look at *Eighteen Days in June* for very long to see how much it is about time and light.

Rob Buelteman shot all of these photographs with a 35mm camera and infrared sensitive film. Though he doesn't say so, it's hard not to think that this choice was itself a metaphor. Infrared film is sensitive to radiation the human eye can't see. It's another way in which these photographs

aren't about how we usually look at things. For
the artist, this may or may not have meant that he
was in search of the invisible, that he was looking
for something in the world that was pitched just
beyond our senses, but that is one of the effects
of these images. And the metaphor gets more
complicated than that. The chlorophyll in plants
reflects almost all infrared radiation—because if it
absorbed it, it would kill the plant. Plants evolved
their green color to ward off red radiation in light.
That's why the reflections in these photographs
are so brilliant. June is still spring in much of the
Coast Range, especially if the spring has been wet
as it was in 1996, and the fluorescent green of
new growth is at or near its most intense. It's
saturated with chlorophyll to provide food for
root growth. The bright whites in these images
are the chlorophyll in the plants throwing off
what would kill them, or, to say it another way, the
film picks up life at its most intense. In shadow,
in filtered light, in cold places, the dark picked up
by infrared film is darker. Skies are darker. The
tingling electrical energy of clouds also reflects
infrared, which may be why the clouds in these
images look so much like living things. Water
absorbs infrared and is at certain angles almost
invisible. Buelteman is able to render, more vividly
than we see it, the dialogue between light and
dark in the physical textures of this specific place.

The specific place—the subject of the photographs—is the Santa Cruz Mountains of the
Coast Range, south of San Francisco. Time,
and grief, and light and dark may be the artist's
preoccupations, but his vocabulary is this
geography, seen with the special set of nerve

endings the small camera and the film stock and the possibilities in the
darkroom gave him. It is territory Buelteman has visited before in *The Unseen
Peninsula,* the book that first drew me to his work and made his reputation
as a landscape photographer, in which his subject was the nearby Crystal
Springs watershed on the San Francisco Bay side of the ridge. In that book
and in this one, I think it helps, looking at the photographs, to have some
sense of the geological and botanical history that Buelteman was walking in.

The Coast Range is a work in progress. It lifted out of the sea something like
thirteen million years ago and it's continuing to rise, according to geologists,
because of the continuous motion of the ocean floor as it bumps up against
and rolls under the plate on which the North American continent floats. It's
an uneasy coast, still in formation along earthquake faults and still working
out its shape in a long conversation with the Pacific Ocean. It's hard to know
what time frame to think in when you walk its hills and canyons.

As the mountains rose, they created California by creating the great
Central Valley, rich with the soils of Sierra run-off. The intimate canyons
in Buelteman's photographs came into being, paleobotanists tell us, when
the ancestors of the current vegetation, Maduro-Tertiary geoflora, to use the
technical term, migrated into the newly formed mountains. The main sur-
vivor of this epoch in the photographs is the horsetail, among the oldest living
things in California. In one of Buelteman's images, *Wake*/Patricia Leighton,
a patch of horsetails, like a miniature forest, is set against an enigmatic
sculpture of three crossed redwood boughs. The horsetails are so new with juice
they are almost ghostly in their lightness. And the off-center boughs of the
sculpture seem to make a brute hieroglyph whose meaning we can't quite read.
Dark and light, certainly, death and life, and the title, which calls up both
wakefulness and funereal starkness, intensifies the riddle, and so does a
knowledge of local botany. The youngest things in this image are also the oldest.

Much more recently, five to eight thousand years ago, the seas rising from
the glacial melt of the last ice age had brought the contour of the coast
to something like its present shape and the weather pattern we live with today
of rainy winters and dry summers and steady visitations of sea fog, neap
tides in January and foggy upwellings in June, had been established and
the aboriginal flora transformed itself into the redwoods and madrones
and bay laurels and coast live oaks and pinyon pines that give California

its characteristic appearance. The ferns came then too, or evolved out of the larger paleolithic ferns; they are the ones that the light seems to dance with in so many of Buelteman's images.

This landscape was first seen, anthropologists guess, by paleolithic hunters ten to twelve thousand years ago. Among their descendants were the Costanoan people. The land evolved with them; they used fire for hunting and also as a farming technique to increase the abundance of some of the staple plants they used for food and medicine and basketry. They weeded and cultivated around the plants they depended on; it was part of their practical knowledge that growing things didn't like to be neglected. The wild places in the Coast Range, that looked to early European settlers like land as the hand of God had brought it into being, had in fact something of its appearance from ten thousand years of Native American gardening.

And something of its appearance it got from Europe, especially the grasses on the hills. The Spanish, when they arrived in northern California, brought with them horses and cattle and sheep and—it is thought—in the fetlocks of the animals, the seeds of Mediterranean grasses. They did so well here, especially the brome and foxtail fescue and wild oat that give Coast Range hillsides their summer gold, that in a generation or two they almost entirely replaced the native bunch grasses. The luminous grasses on the bare hillsides in Buelteman's photographs are, like us, recent arrivals to these shores. To this last transformation of the Coast Range vegetation, we have added only a grace note here and there in the last hundred and fifty years.

Most notable in these photographs is the foxglove, a European garden plant escaped into the wild. It's instantly recognizable by its spires of white and purple bell-shaped flowers. Foxglove likes disturbed ground. You can walk through whole avenues of it, head-high, on old paths on moist slopes near the sea. It's probably not more than a hundred years old as a wild plant, but in May and June it gives the Coast Range forests one of their most spectacular and characteristic effects. In *Mona Lisa's Grave*/Mark Oliver, Buelteman again sets a plant against a sculpture: the bright bells of the foxglove, rising from leaves on the forest floor, lean toward Mark Oliver's black tombstone-like sculpture while another cluster of bells seems darkened by the sculpture's presence. The riddle here seems to lie

in the small square of—what is it?—tin? tacked to the gravestone, but it adds something to the poignancy of the image to know the flowers have escaped from gardens, from the human impulse to make beauty, to wander in these hills.

Add to this, in the vocabulary of these photographs, the marks of the specifically human world: roads, old farmhouses, fenceposts, and the sculptures of the artists of the Djerassi Program who have made their own marks in this palimpsest, and you have the world Buelteman went into with his camera. He has made of its many elements a complex and moving work: grief, the artist's search for light and life, mourning and bereavement which seems to have meant in this case giving back the seen world to lost loved ones, the layerings of time in the greys and silvers of the darkroom work and of the place itself, the old volcanic and primordial time of the configuration of the hills, the post-glacial time of the redwood forest and the luminous oaks, the crosshatchings of time in grasses and ferns and wildflowers each with their own story to tell. And our part of the story: roads, fenceposts and farms. They mark an older human presence and mark what is implicit in all the photographs, the unseen continuous pressure from suburban sprawl. This gives to the black bands of film that frame the images another level of meaning. Then, in the sculptures set among these scenes, there is a record and a celebration of the company of artists that the residency provided. And, finally, a record of the time and place and freedom to work Buelteman was given and has given back to us as art.

—Robert Hass, May 2000

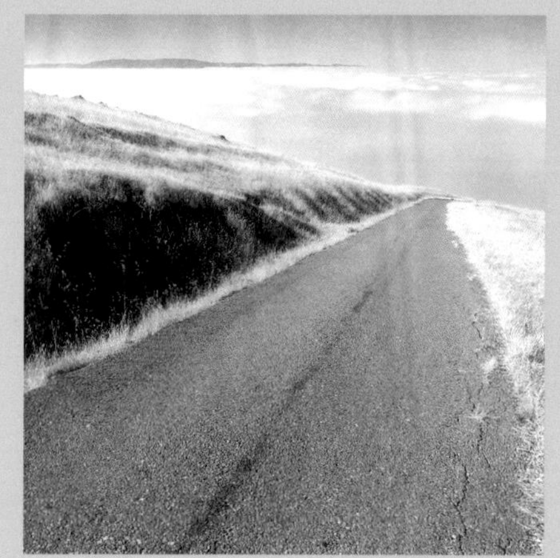

O beautiful

      Darkness and silence, the two
      eyes that see God; great staring

Eyes

— Robinson Jeffers, 1942

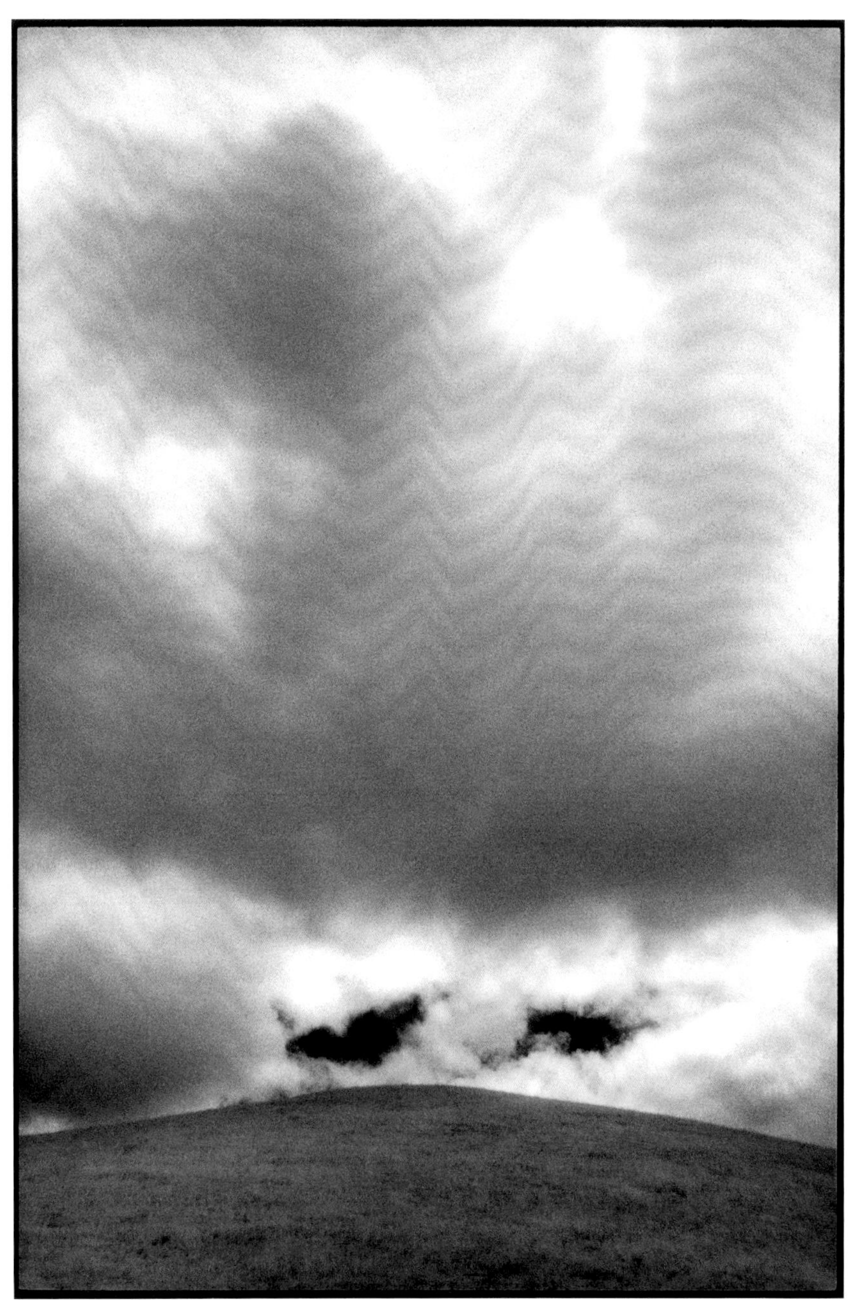

Plate 1
Bare Hill and Clouds

P L A T E 2
U N T I T L E D / M A U R O   S T A C C I O L I

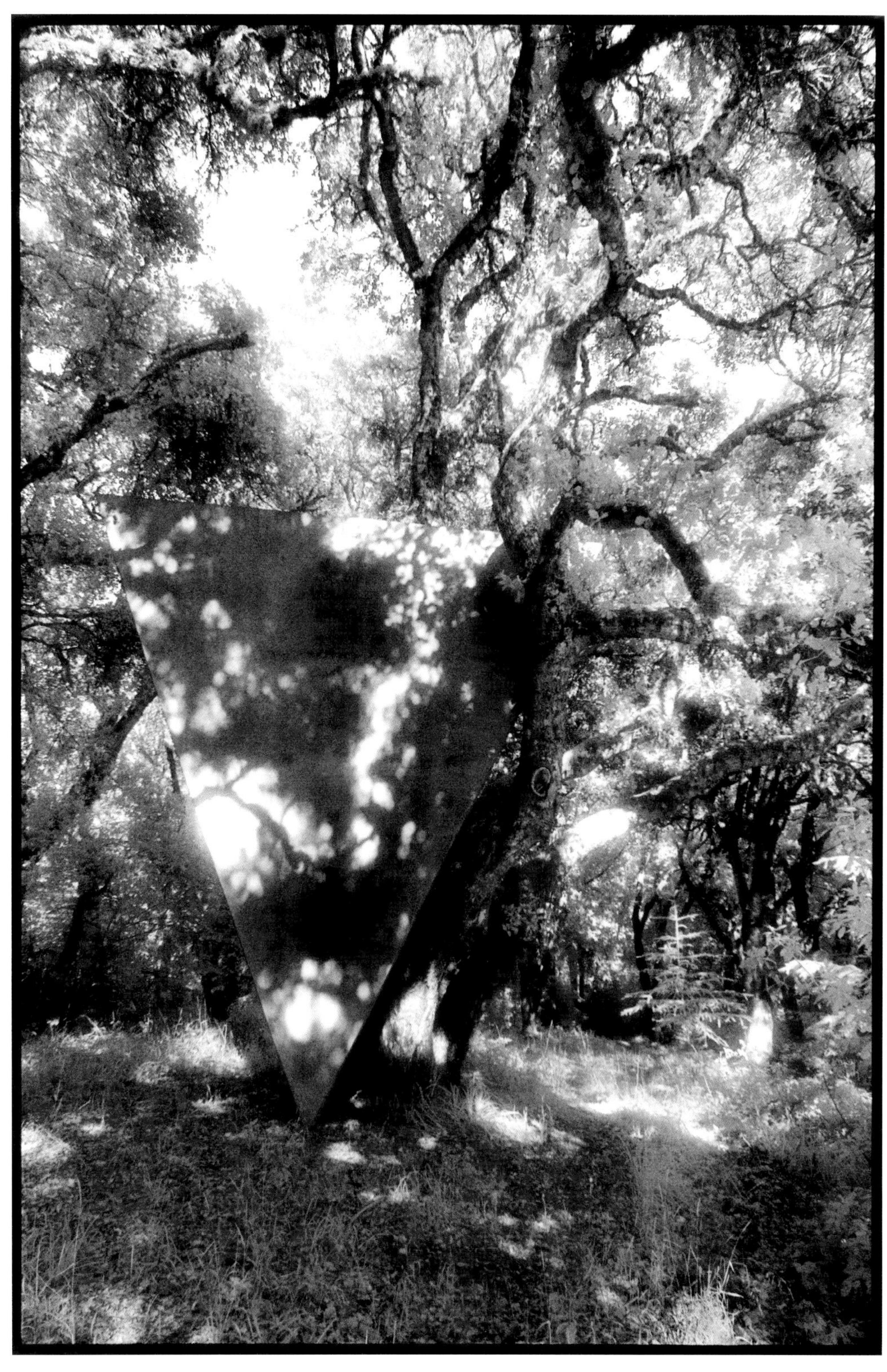

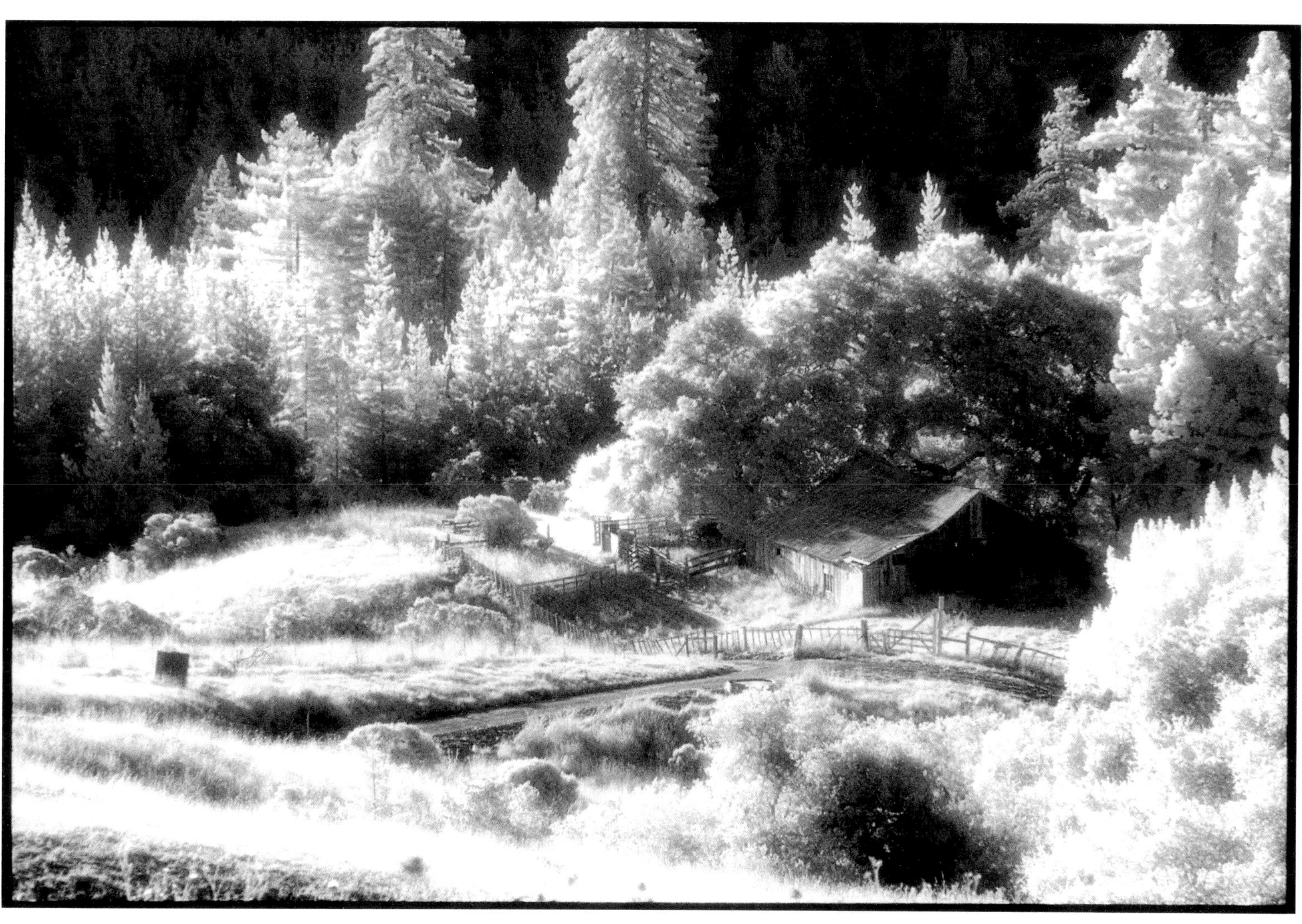

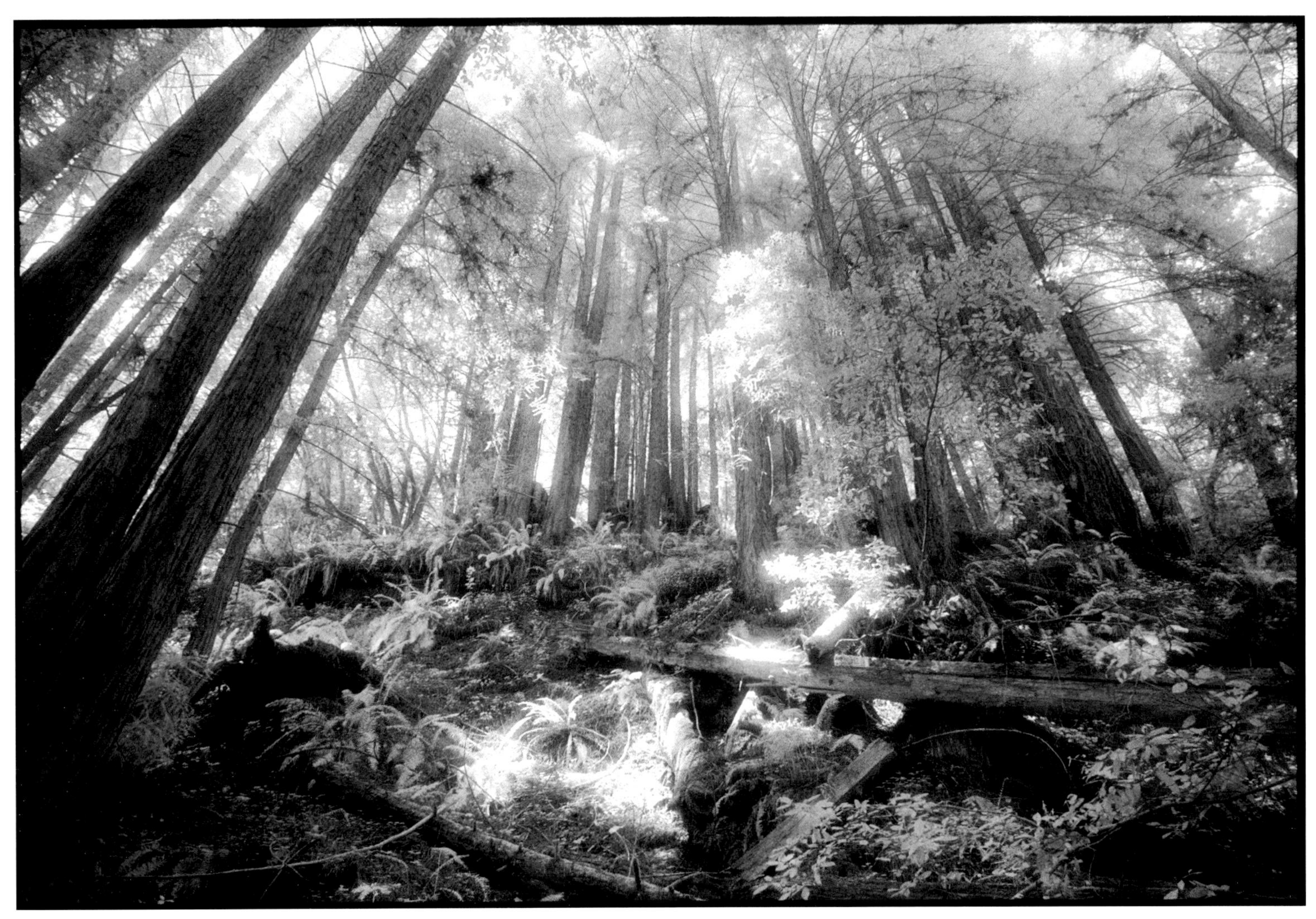

Plate 6

Cascade, Harrington Creek

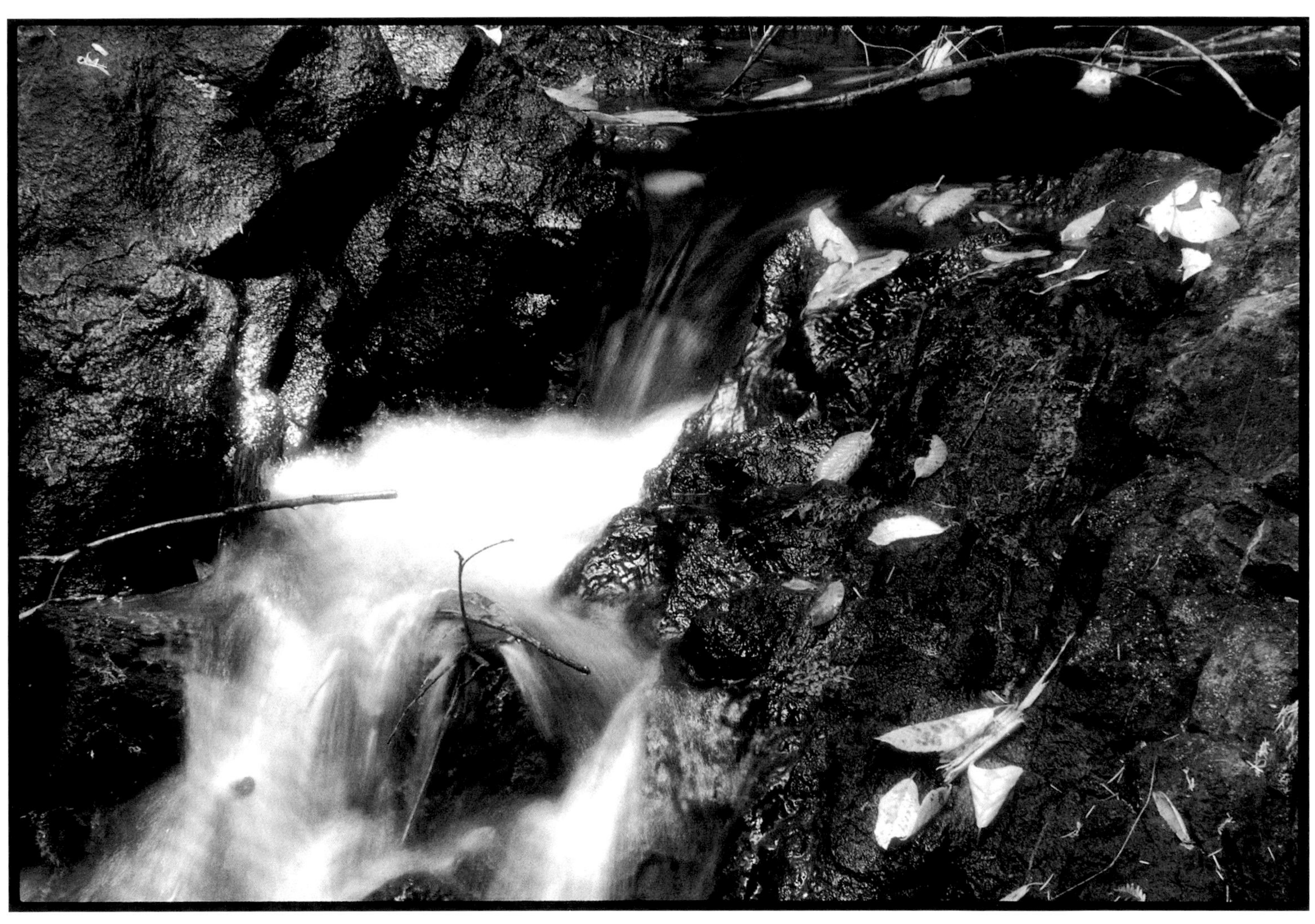

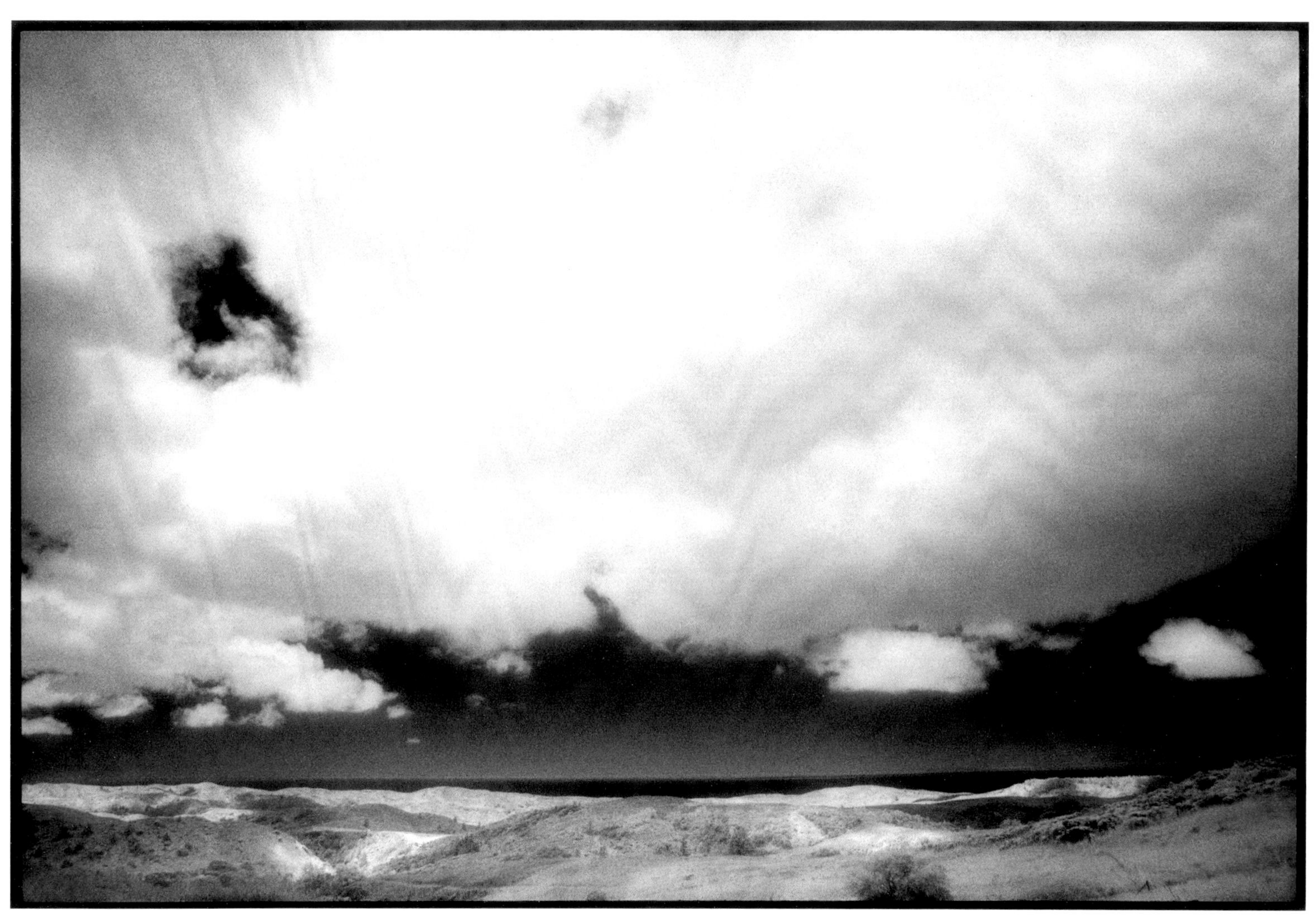

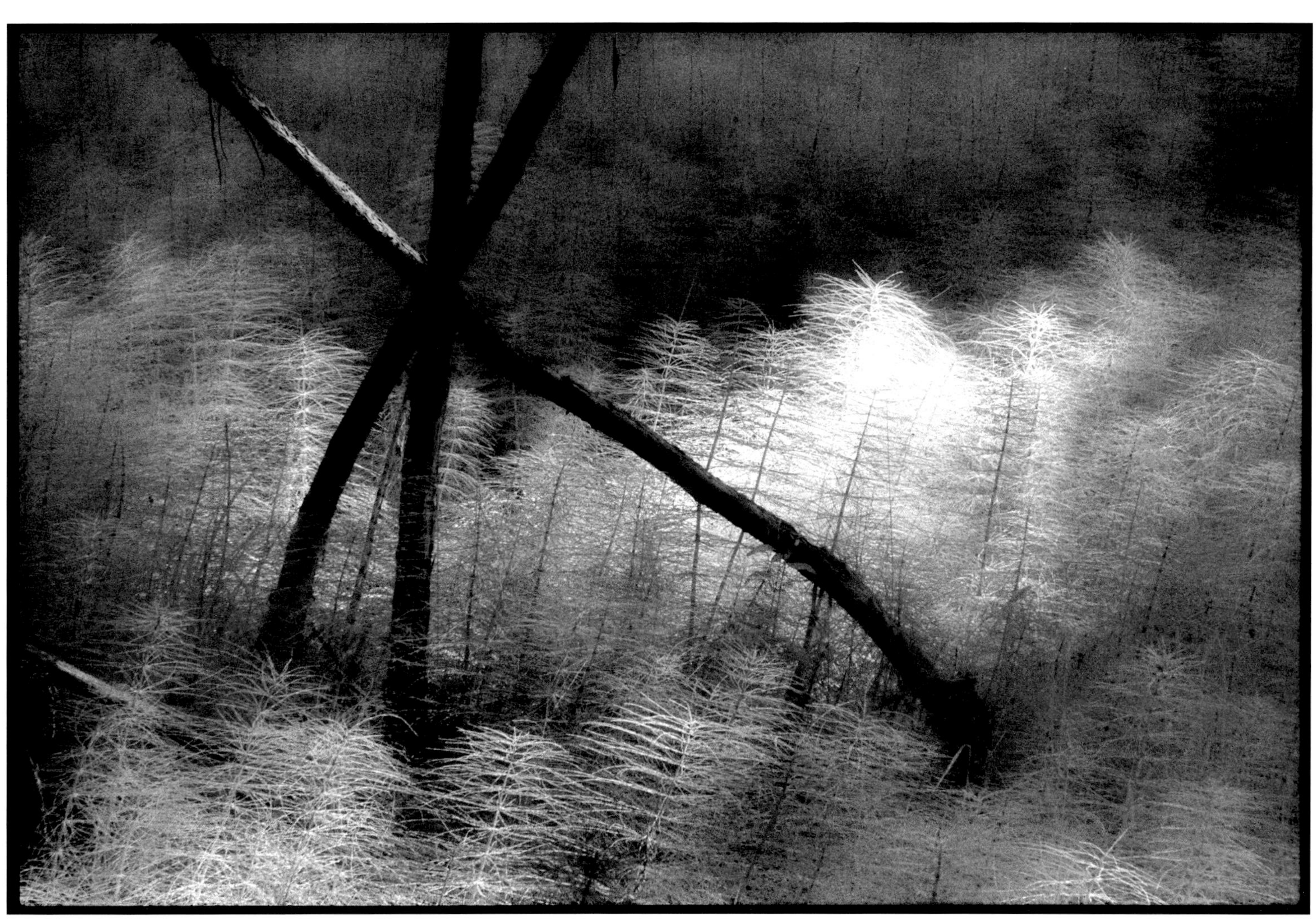

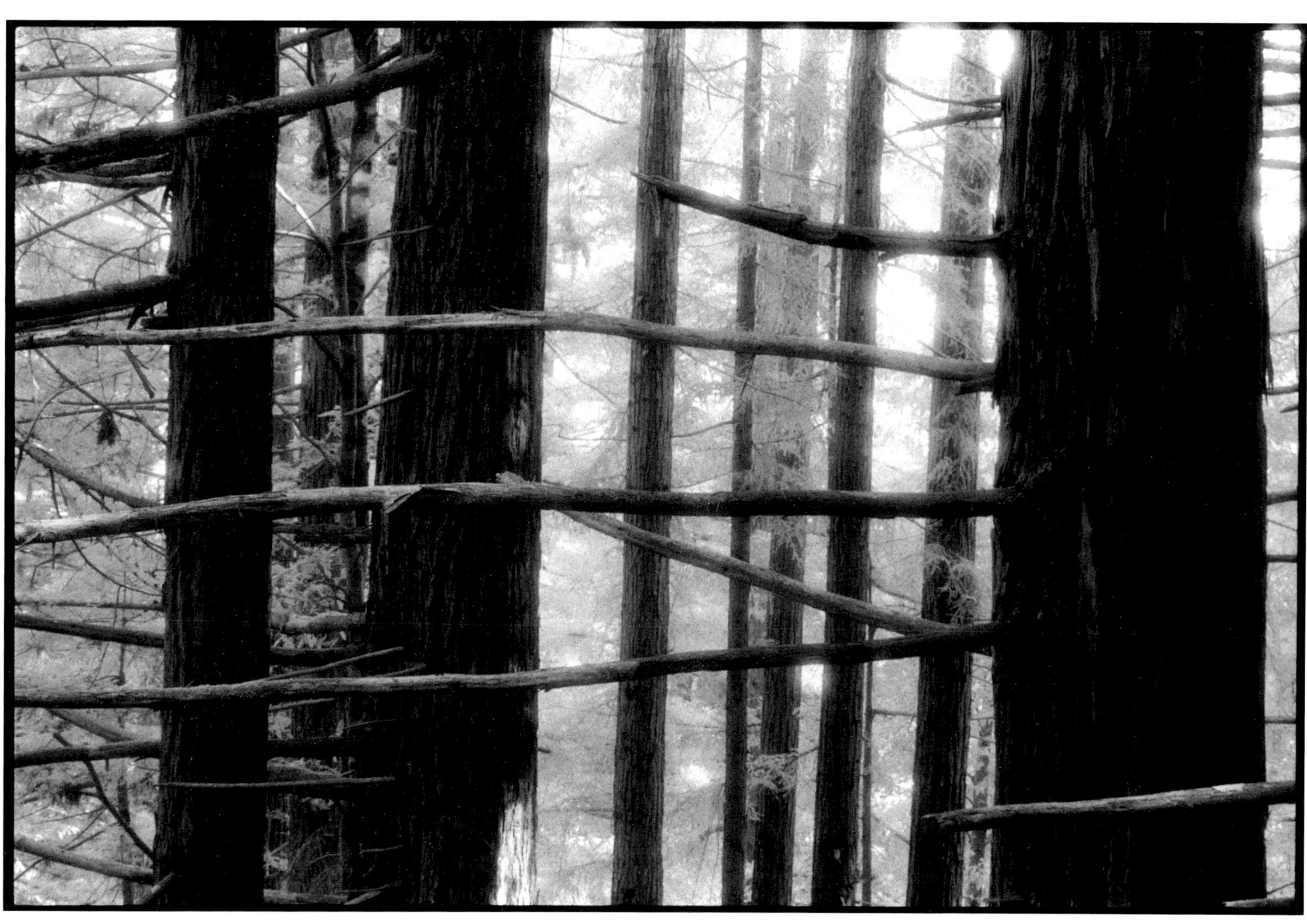

P L A T E 10
G R A C E

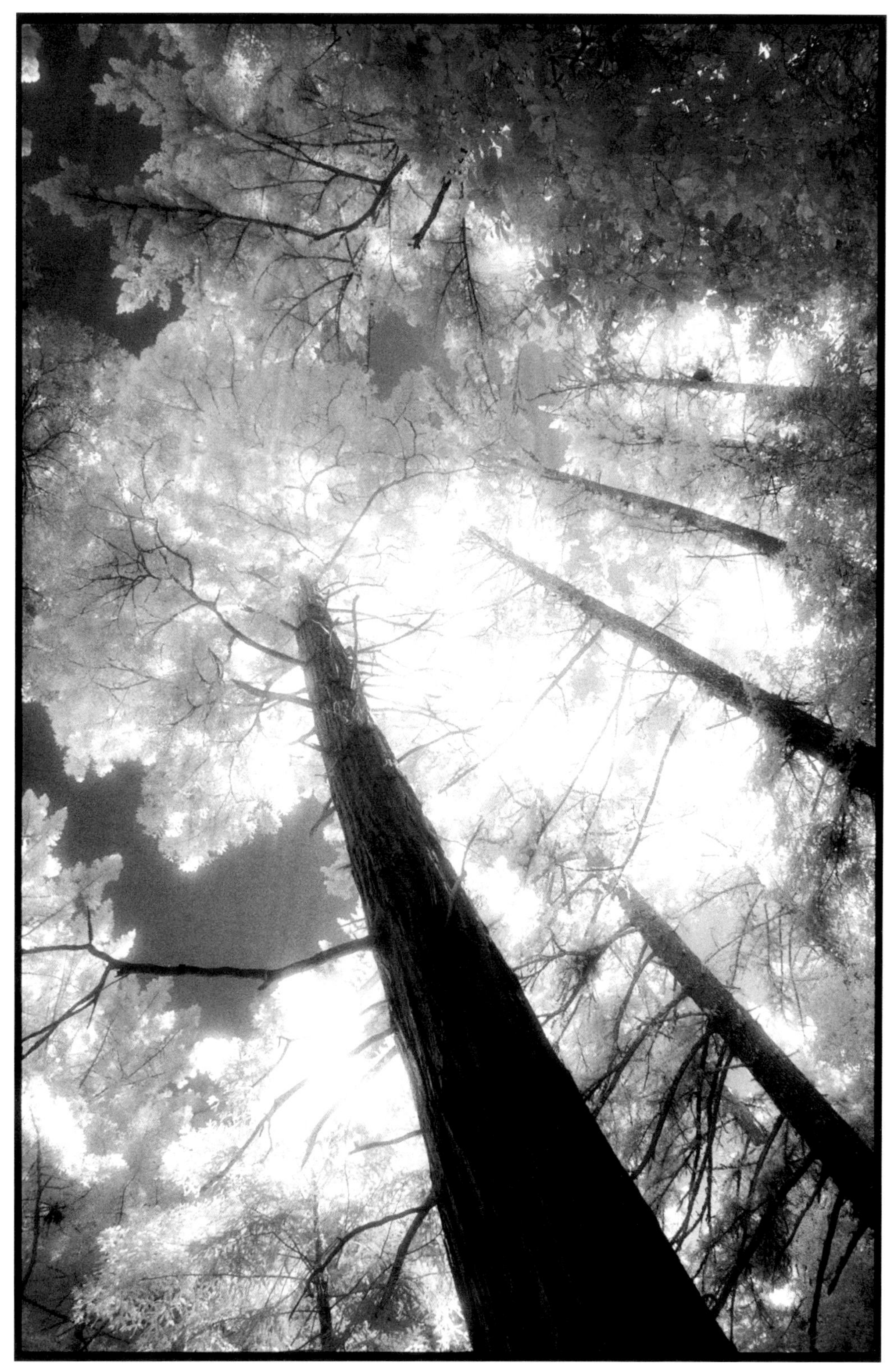

Plate 11
Witness

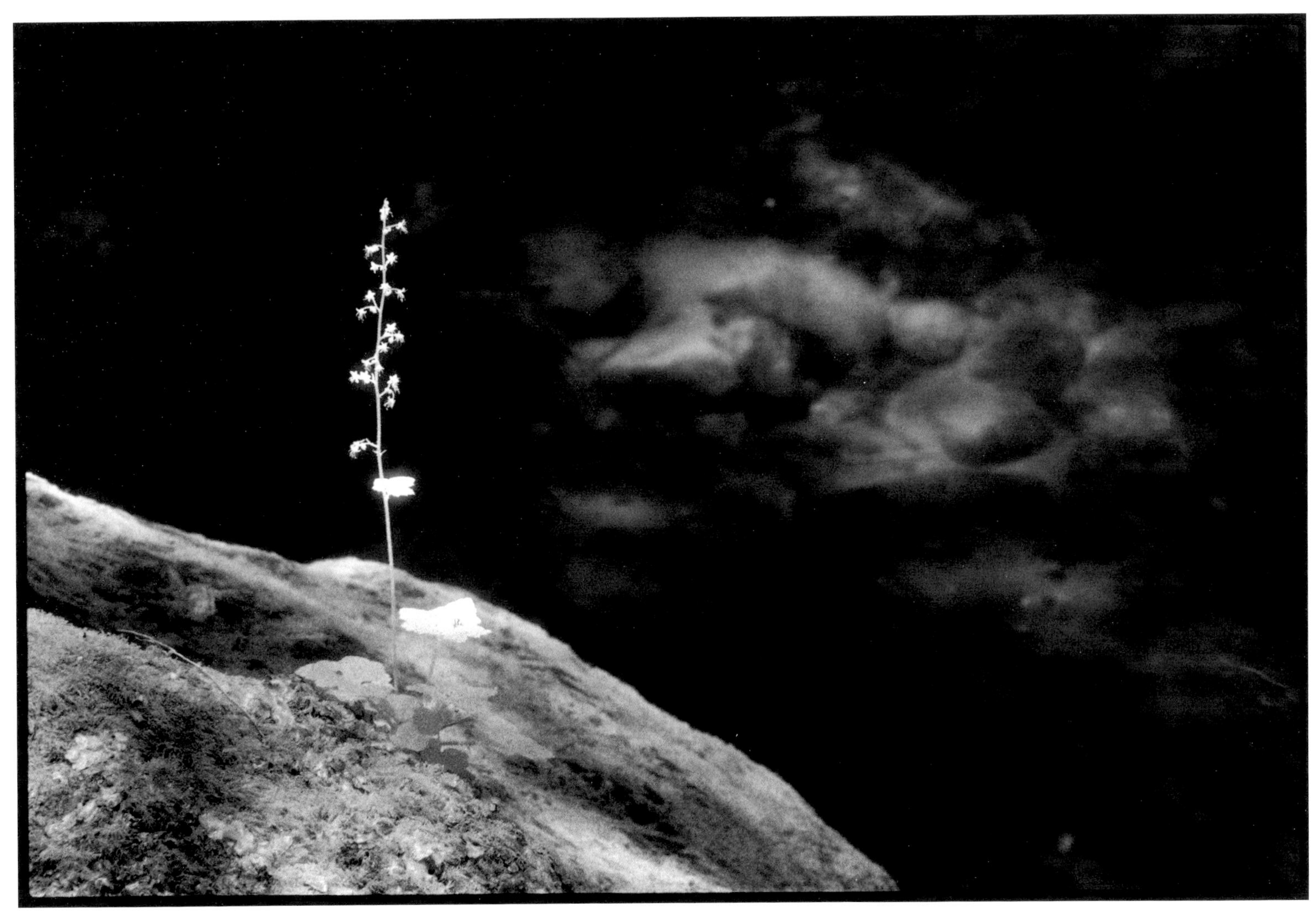

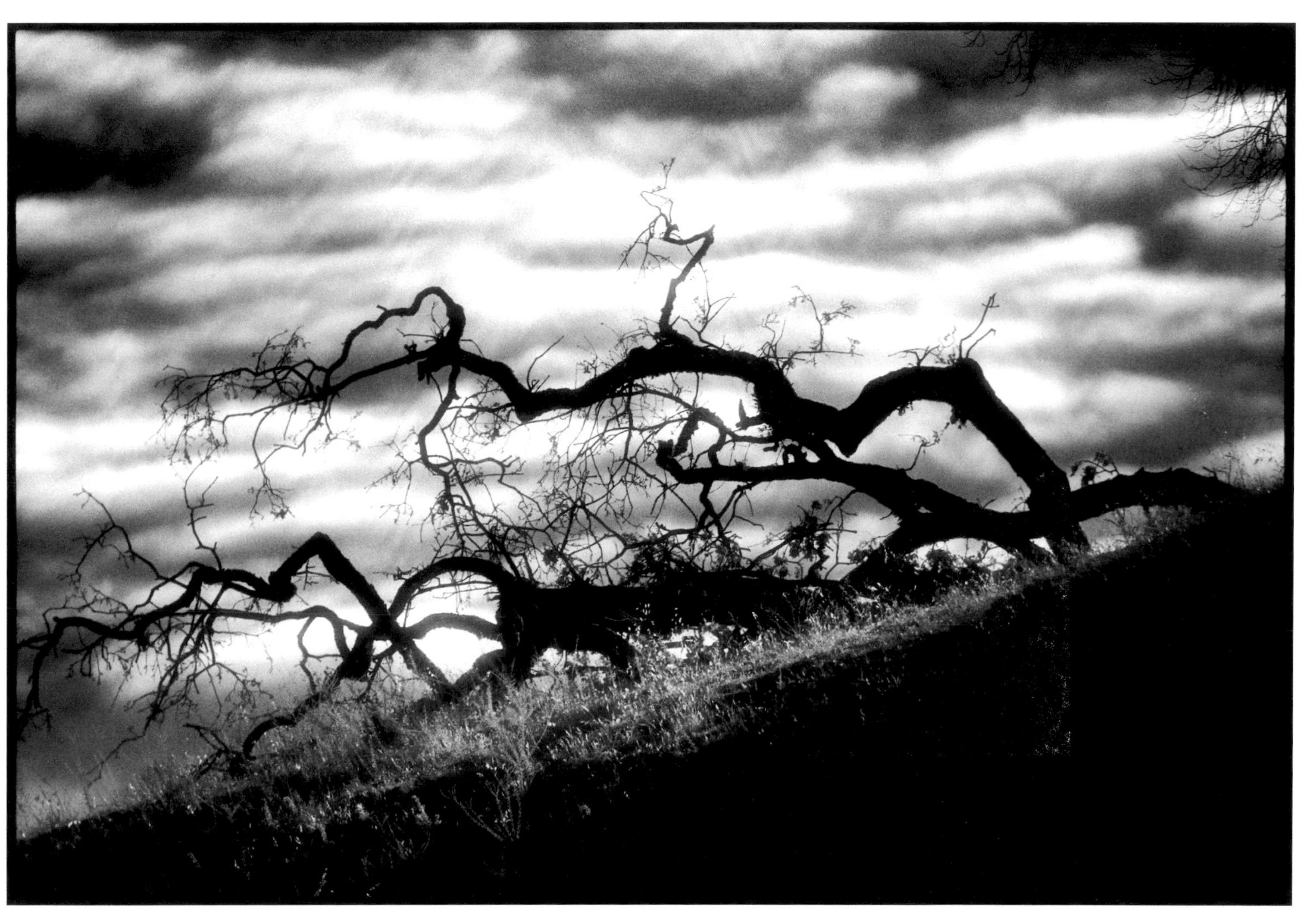

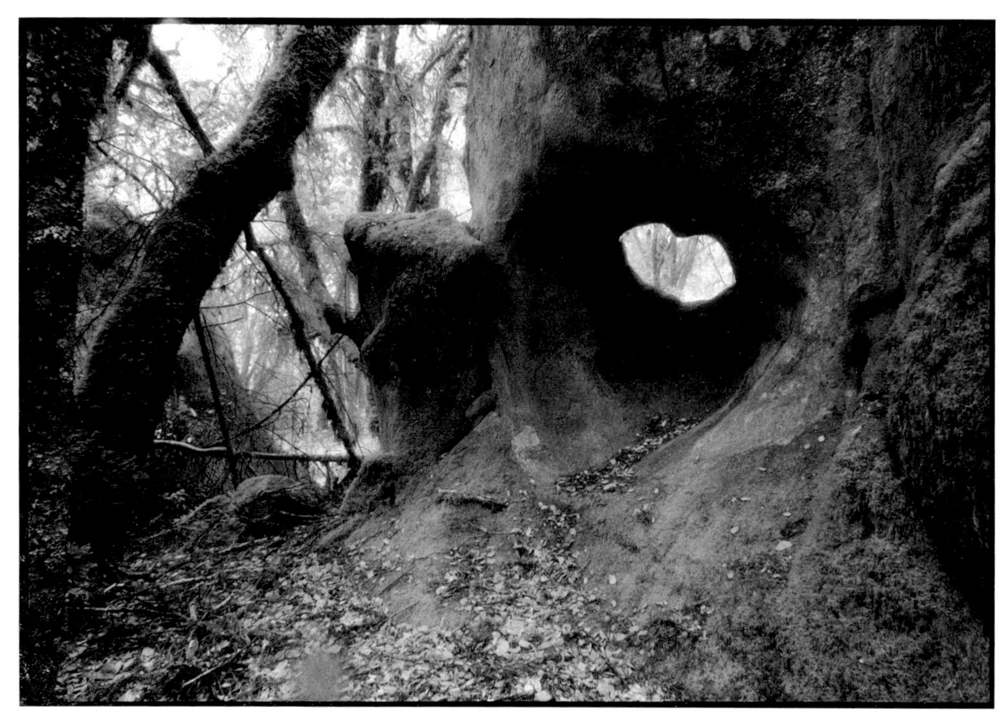

Plate 13
Allen Lookout

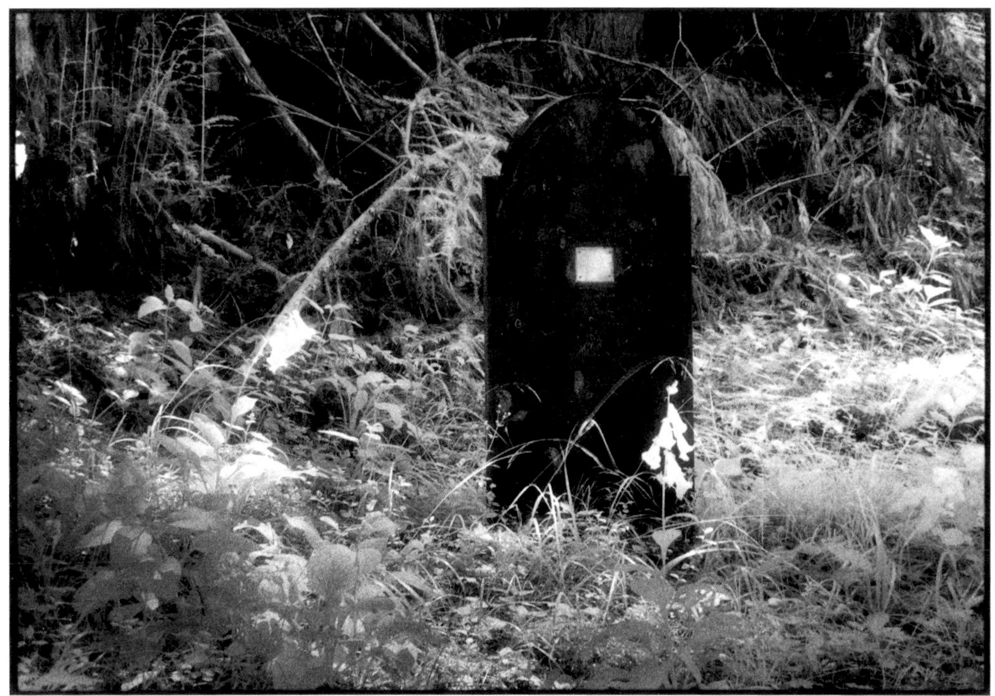

Forest Grotto

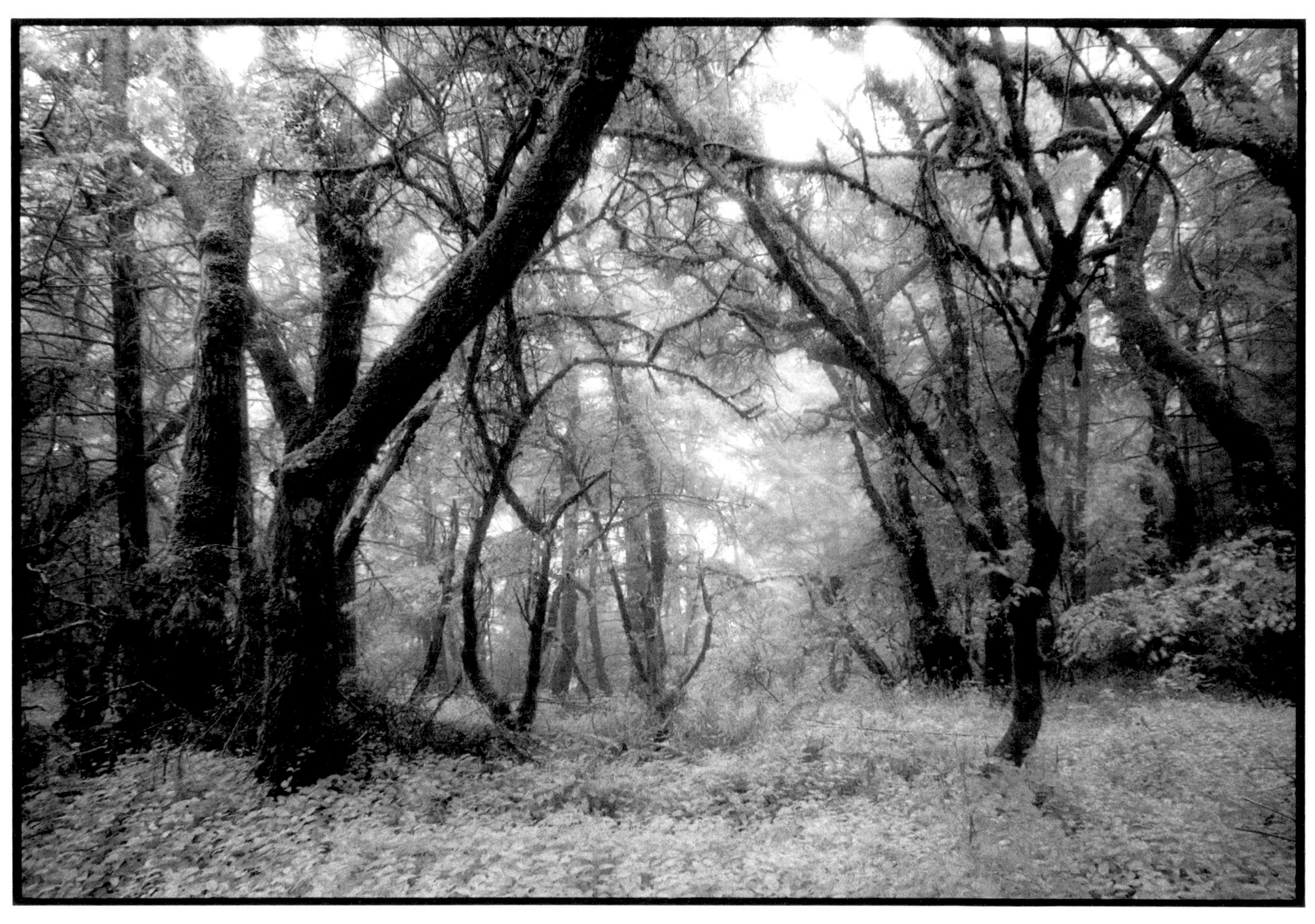

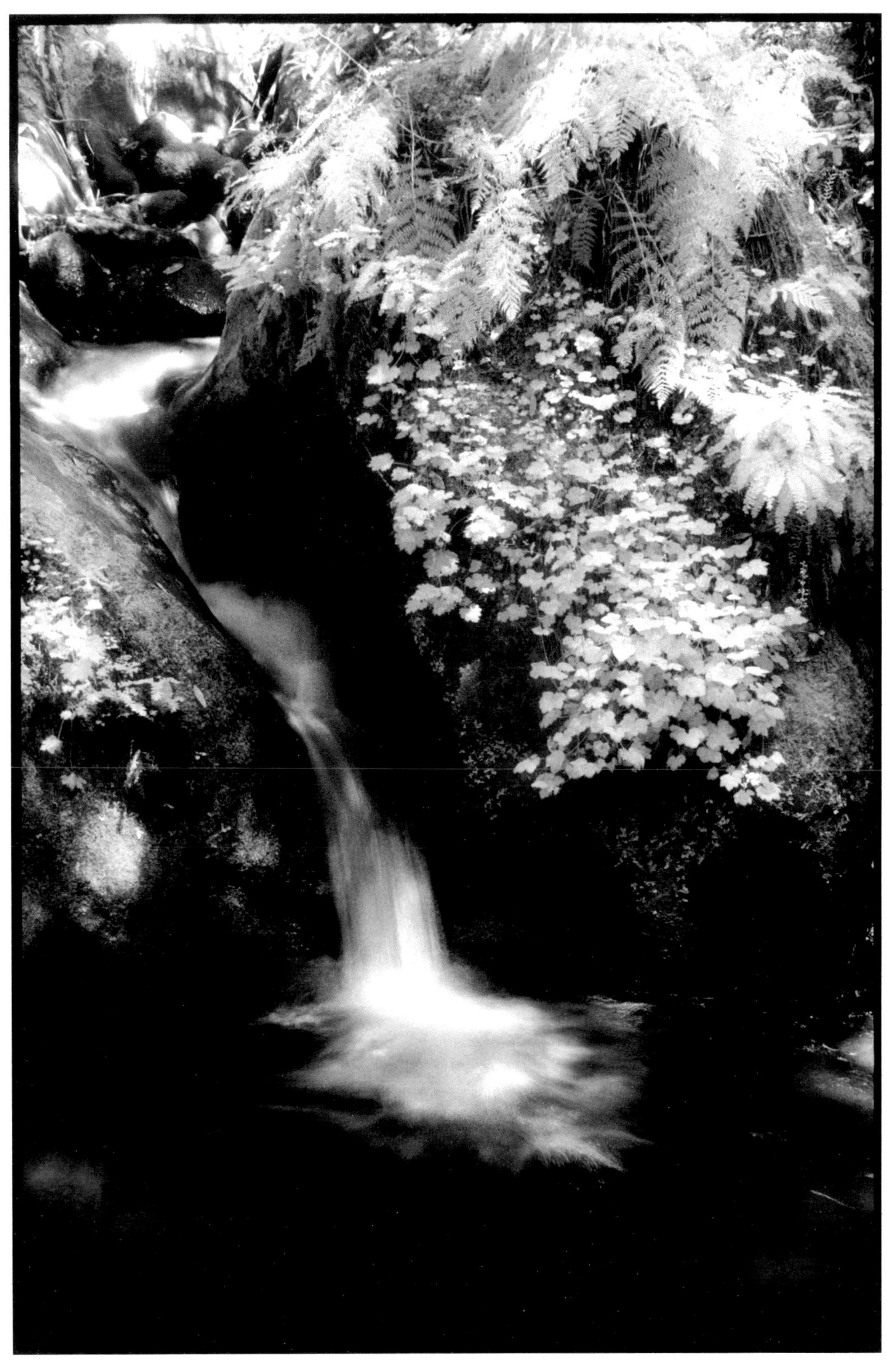

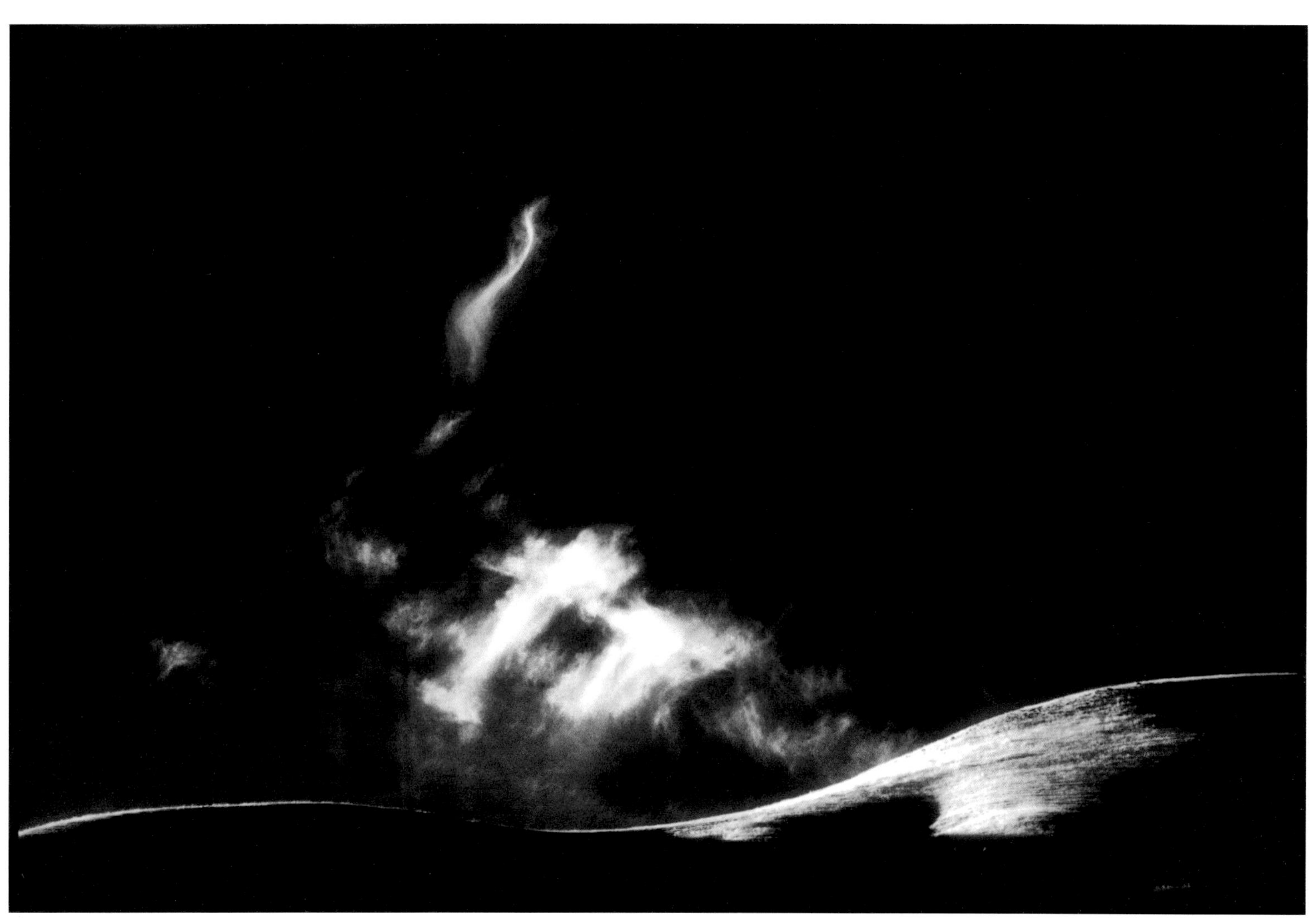

PLATE 18
PASSAGES

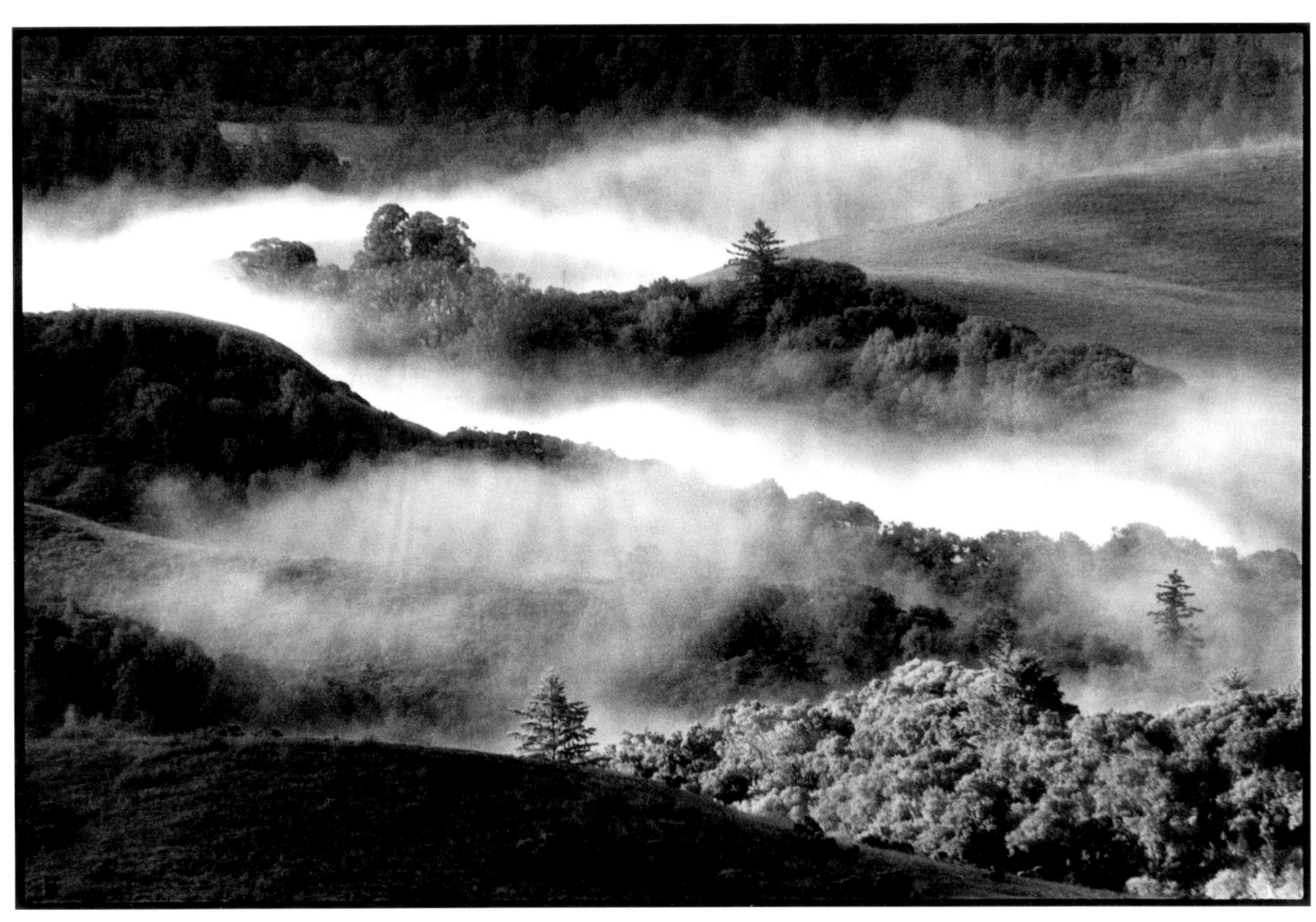

Plate 19
Ferndance

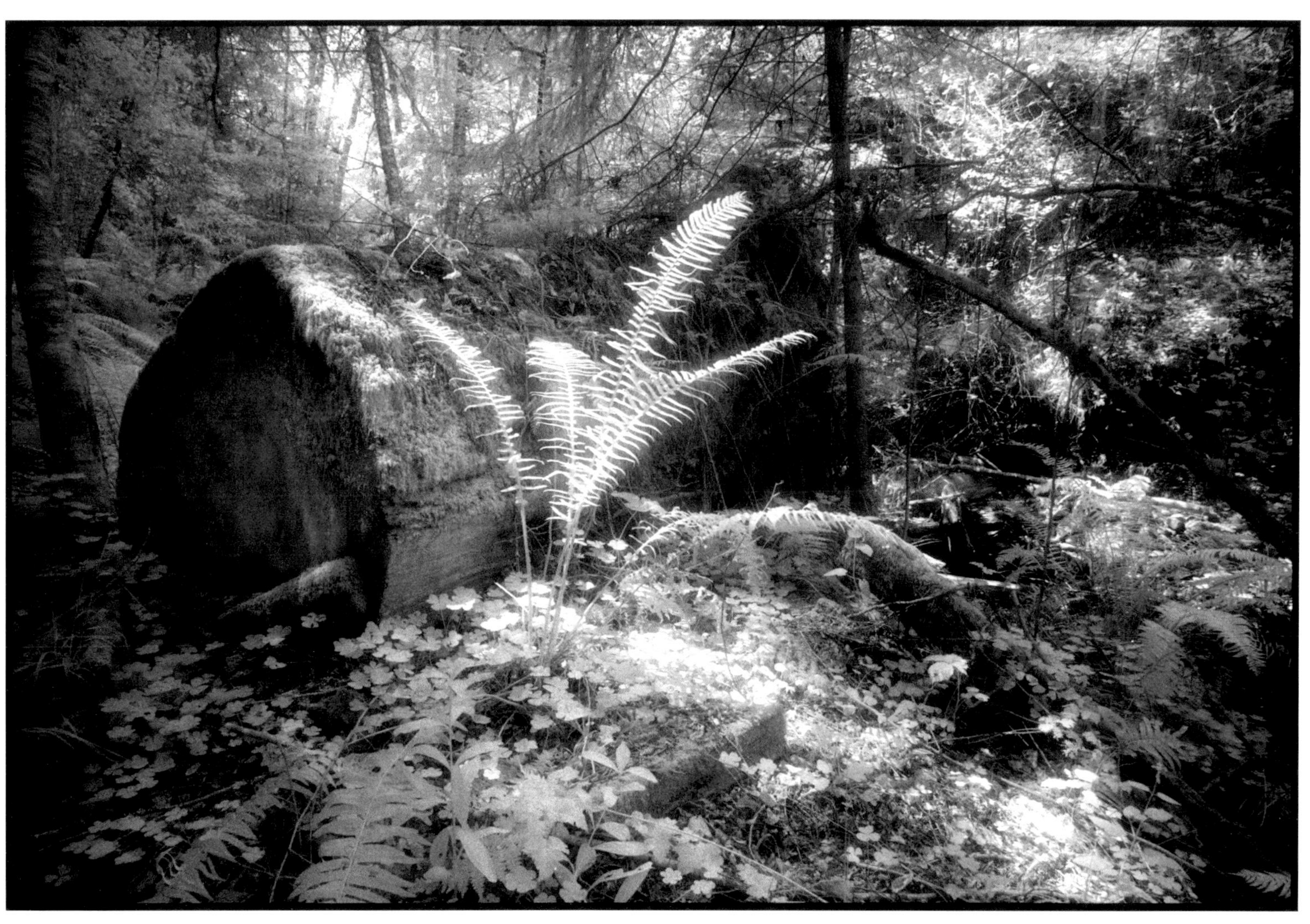

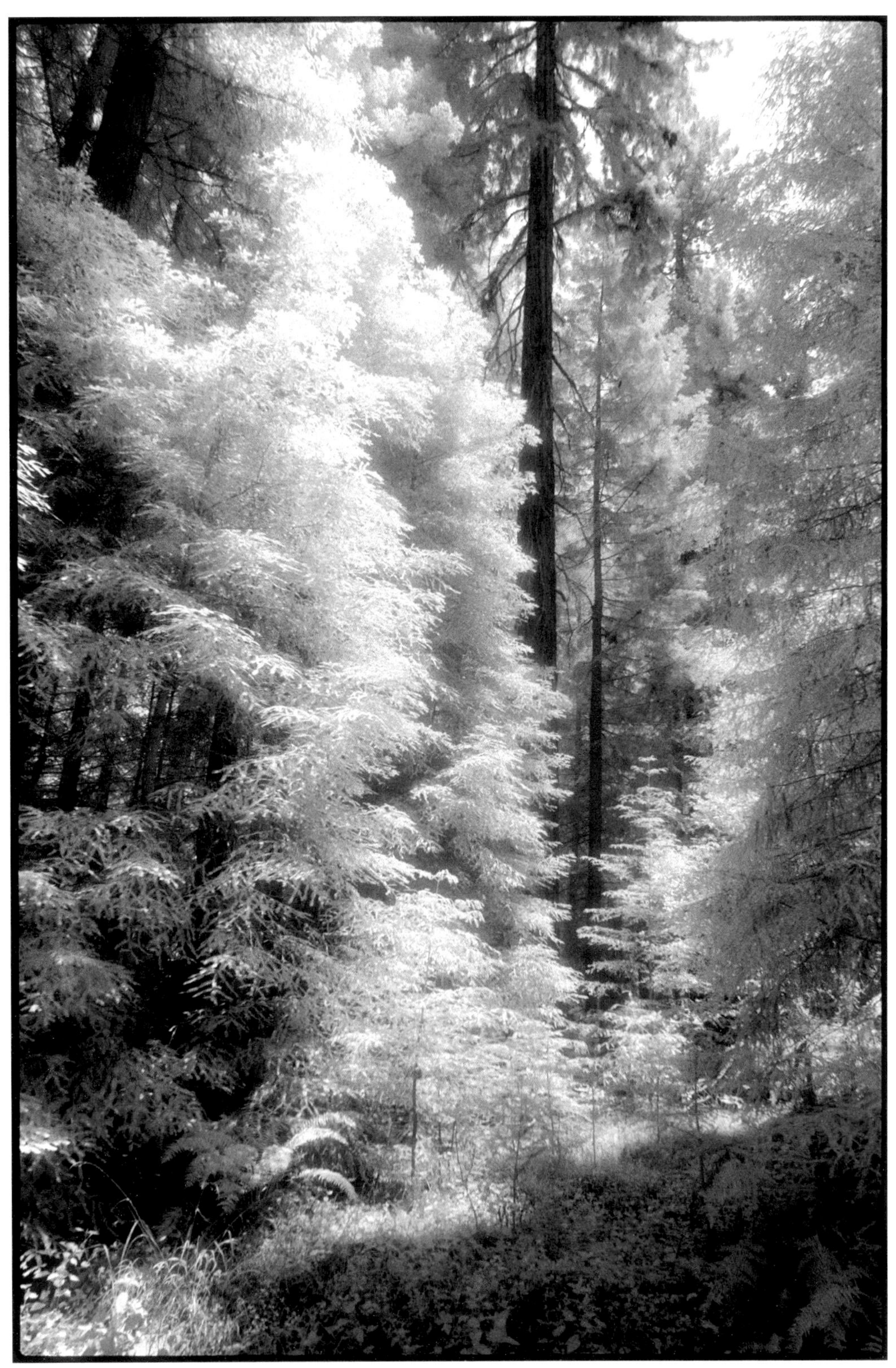

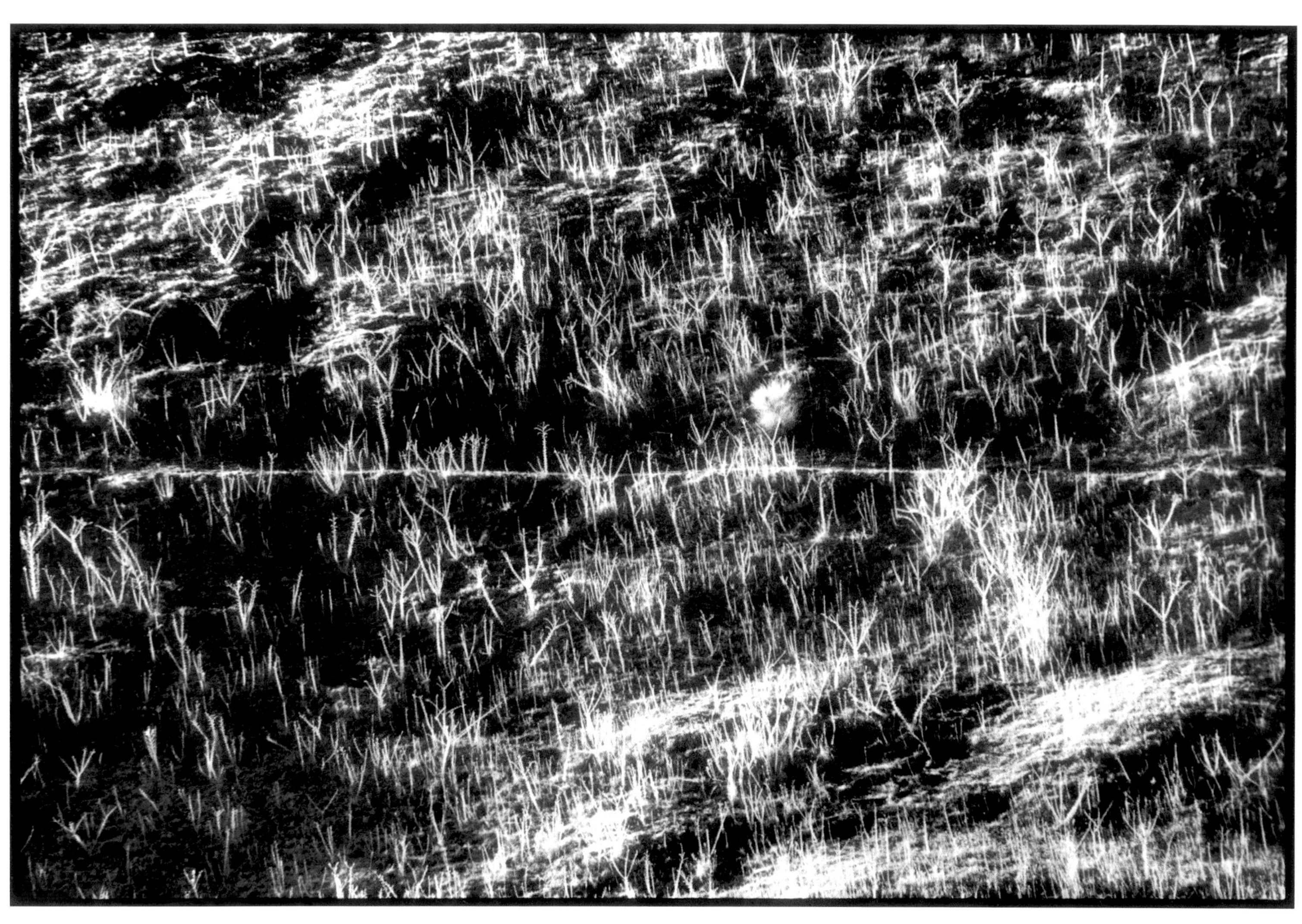

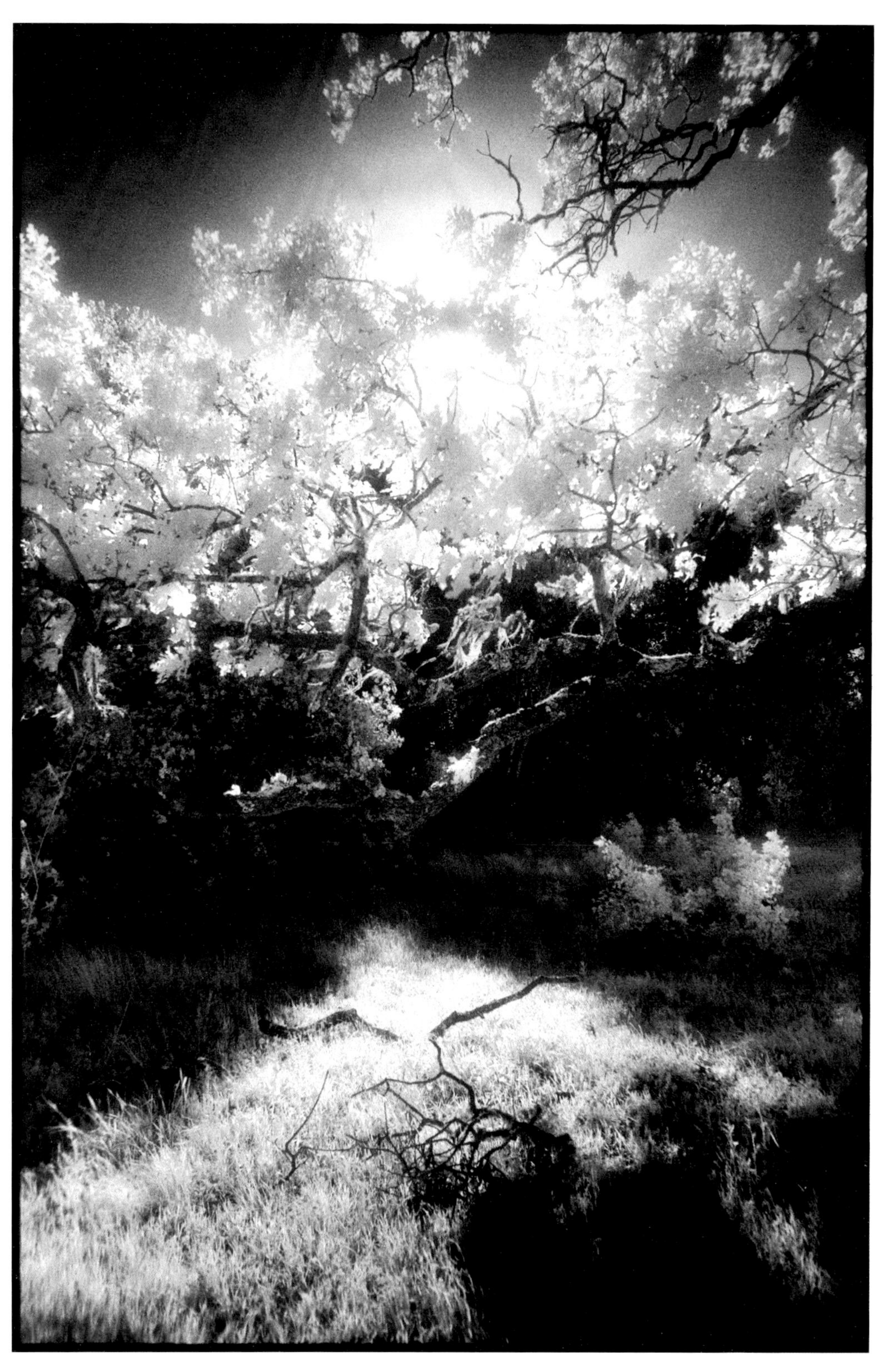

PLATE 23
Double L
Excentric Gyratory/
George Rickey

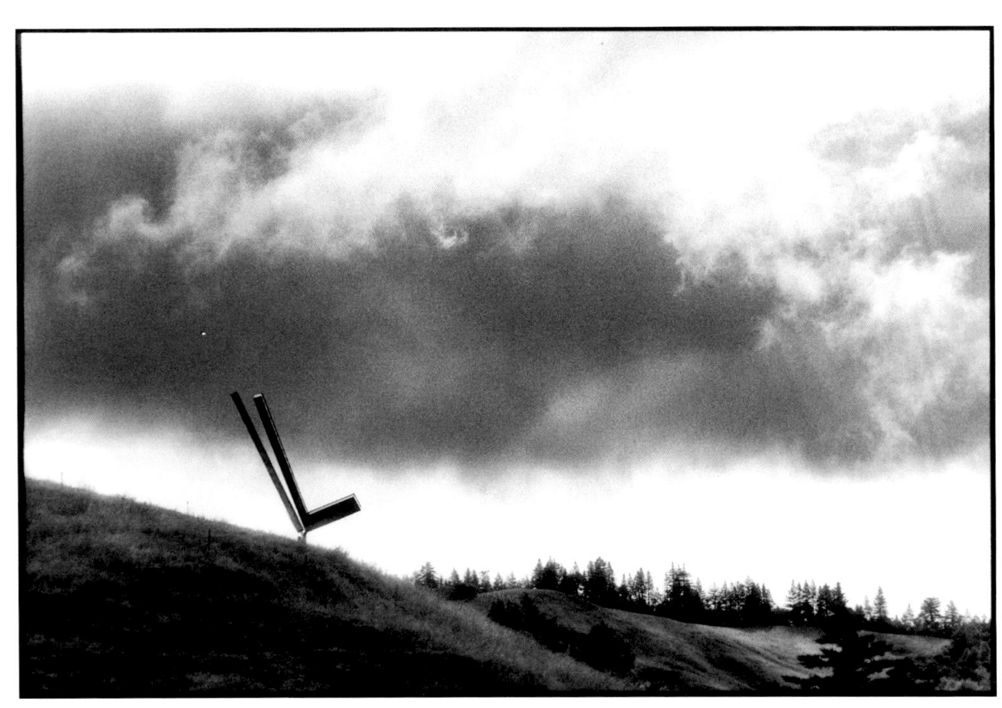

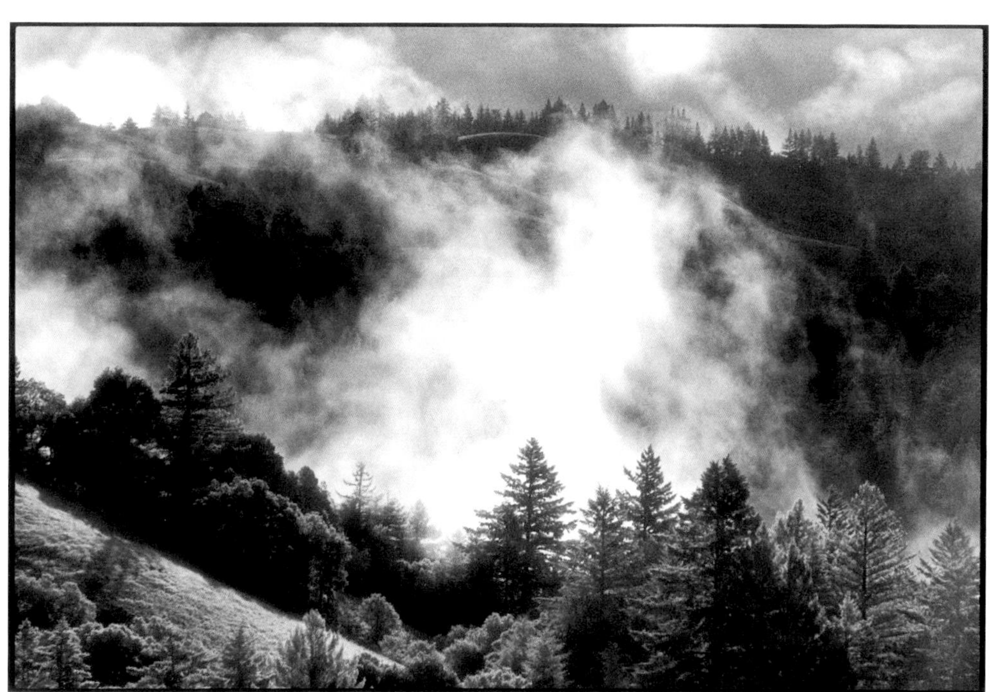

Plate 24
Carl's Canyon

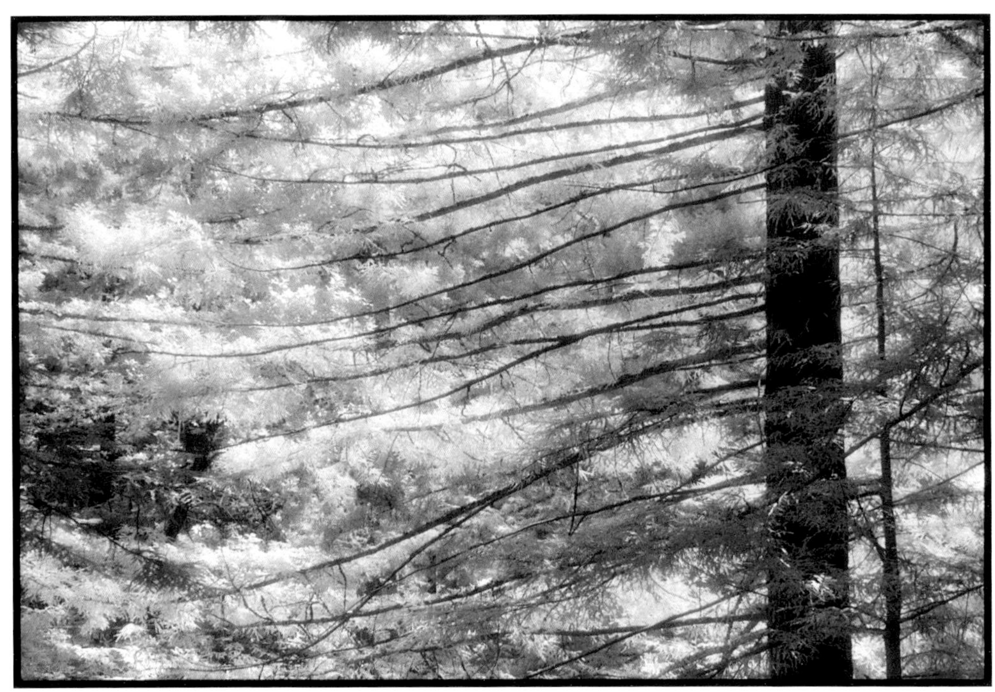

PLATE 25
SEQUOIA SEMPERVIRENS

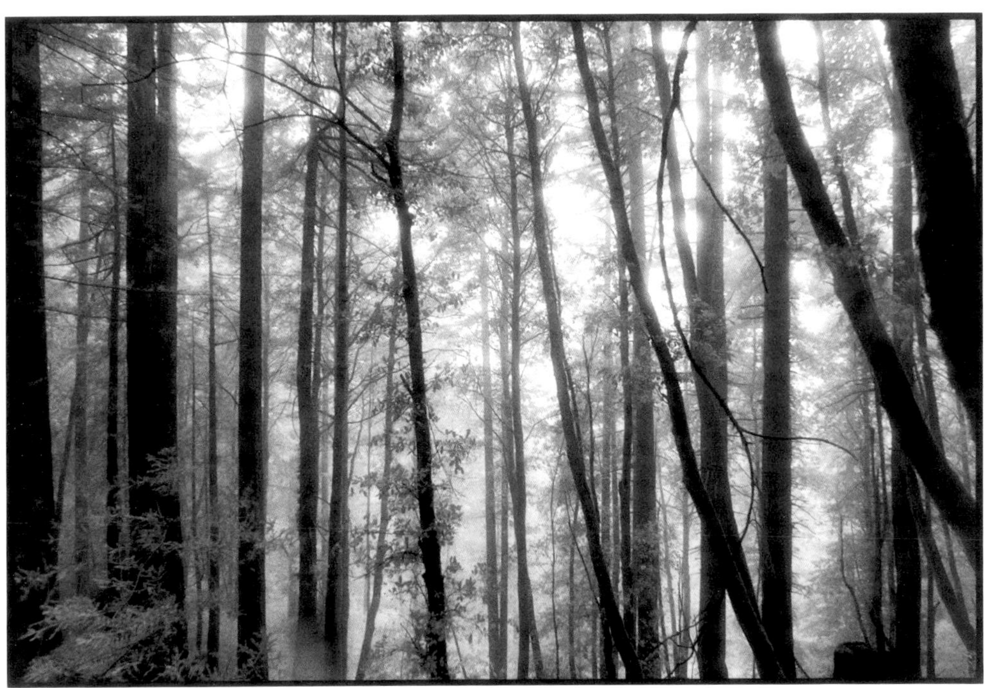

Plate 26
Mountain Fog

Plate 27
Sylvan Steps/David Nash

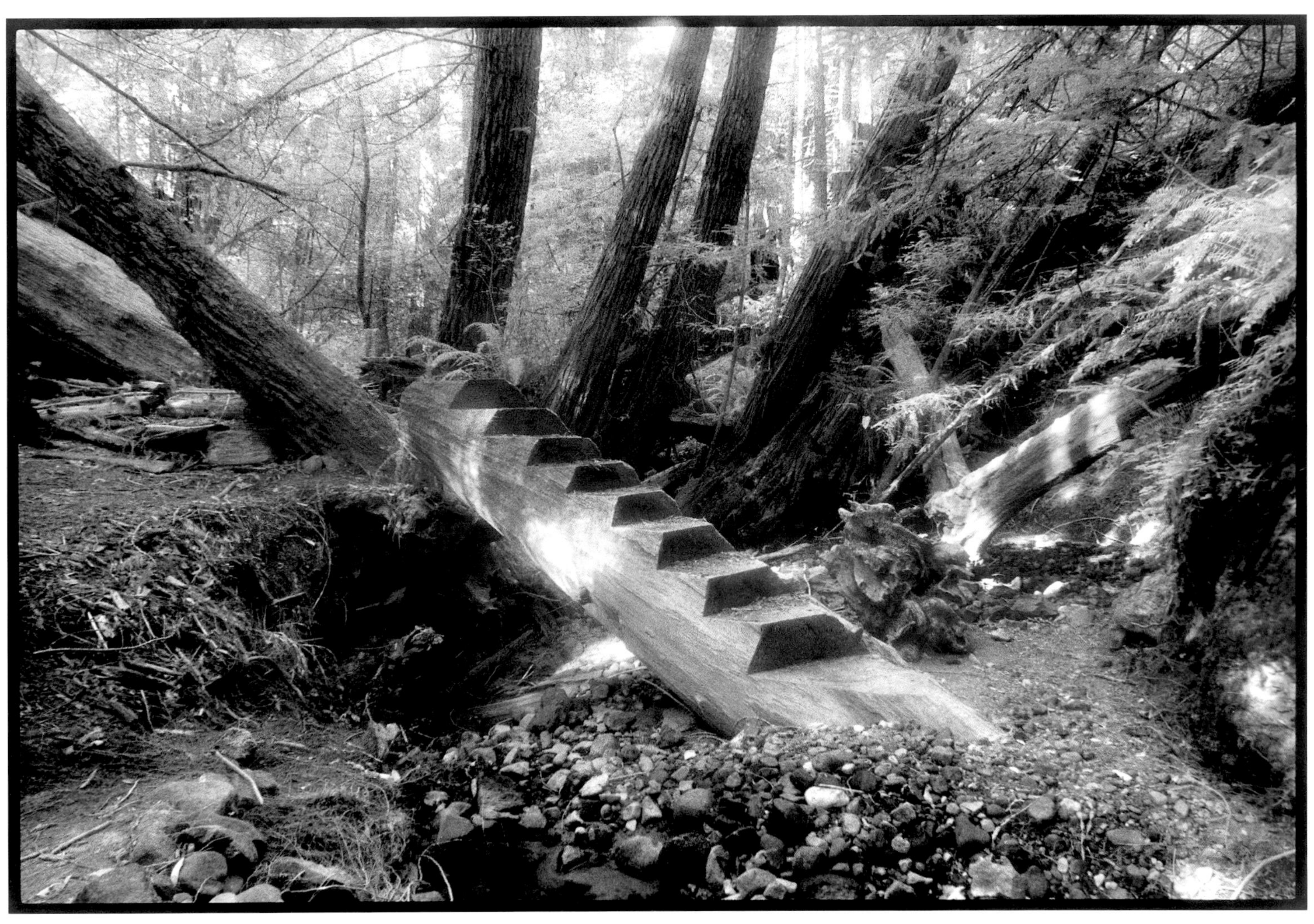

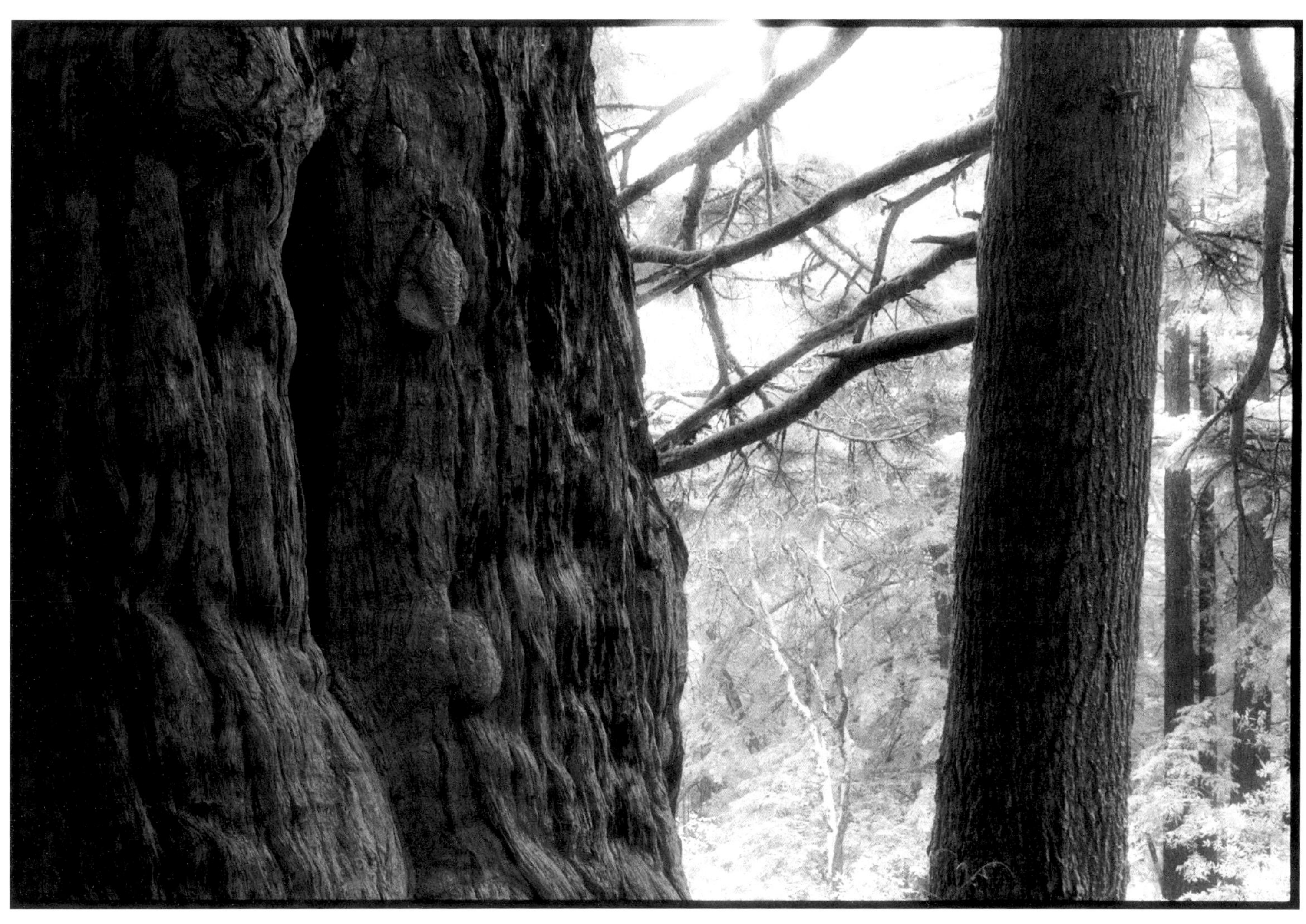

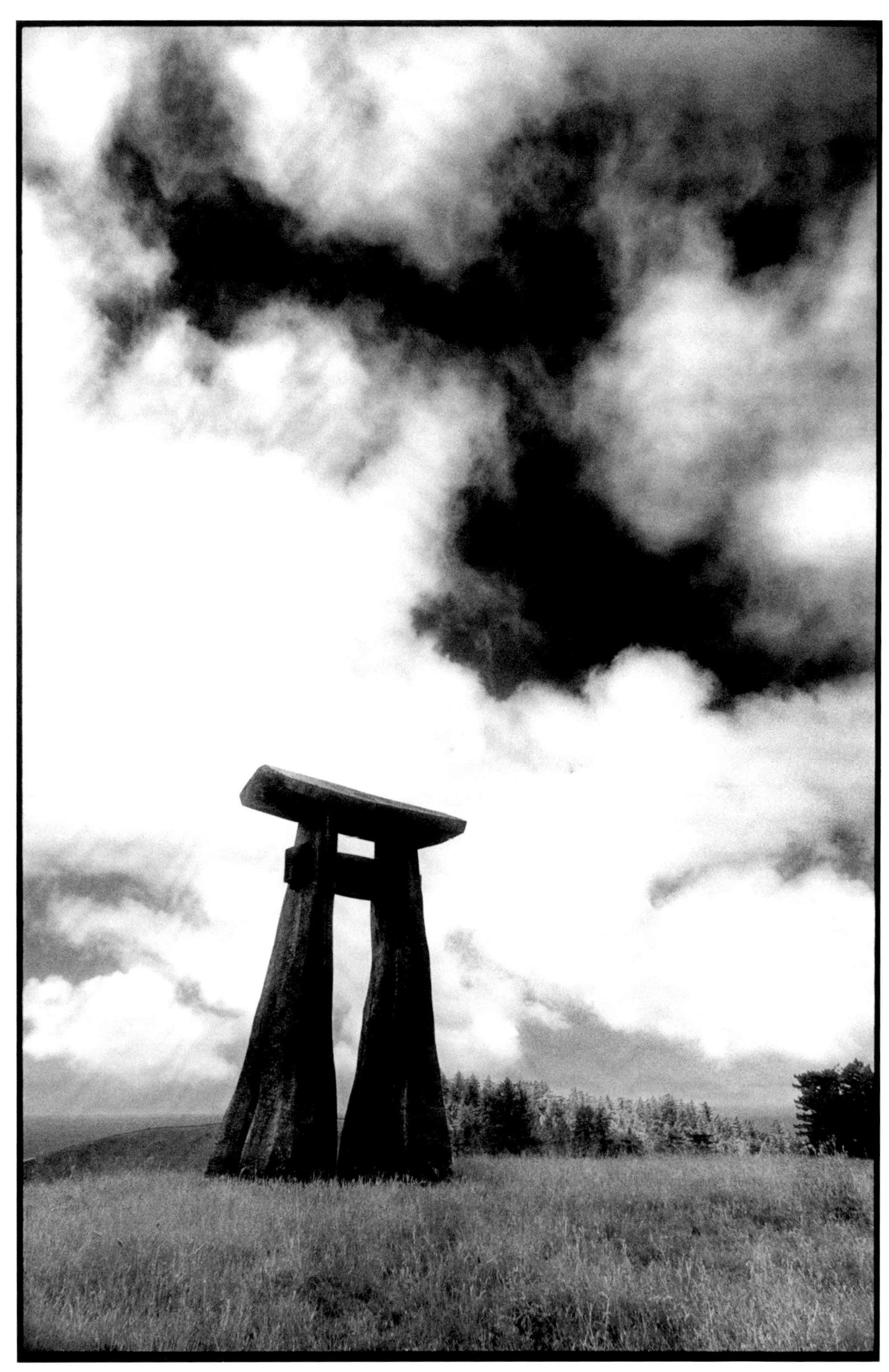

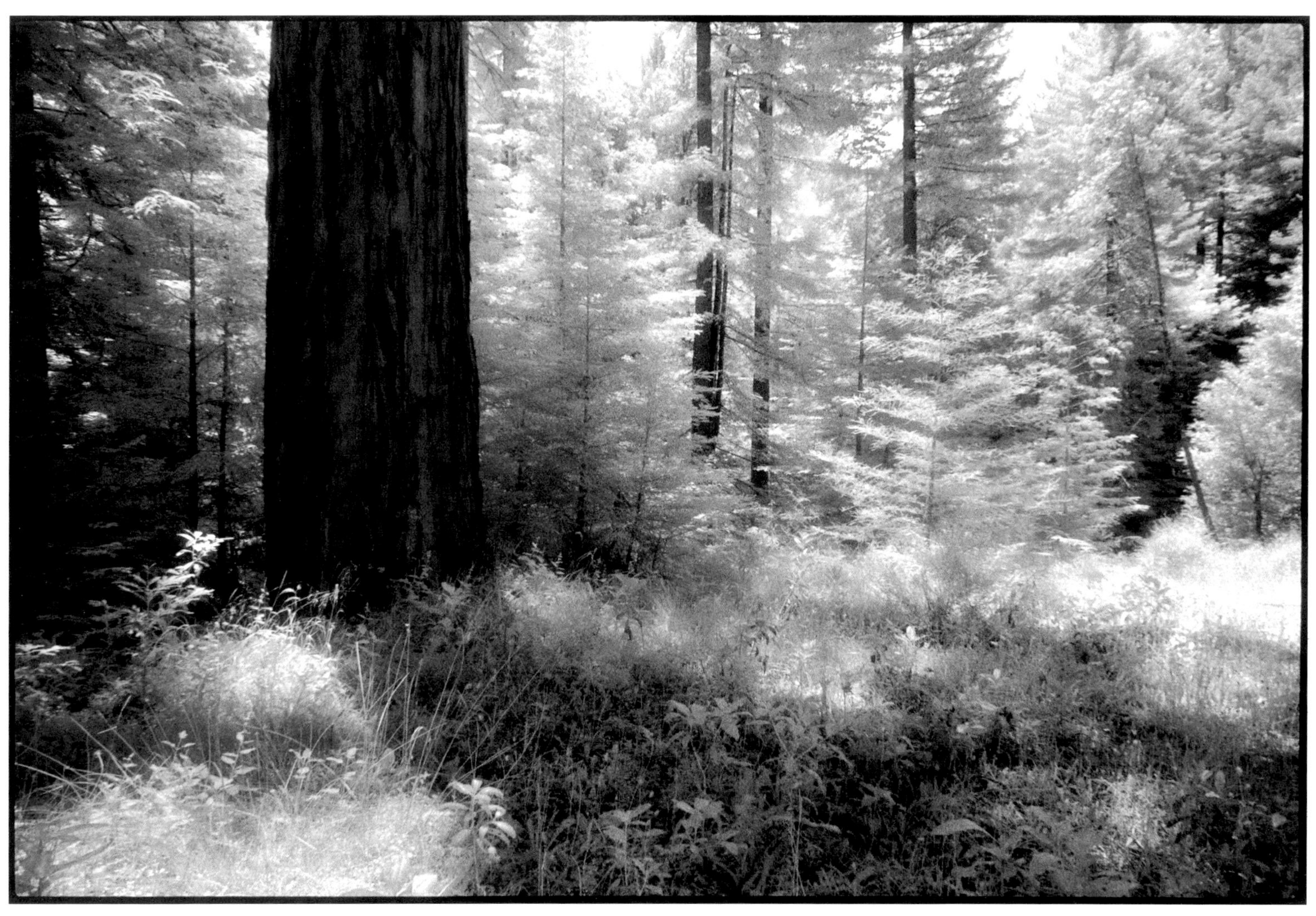

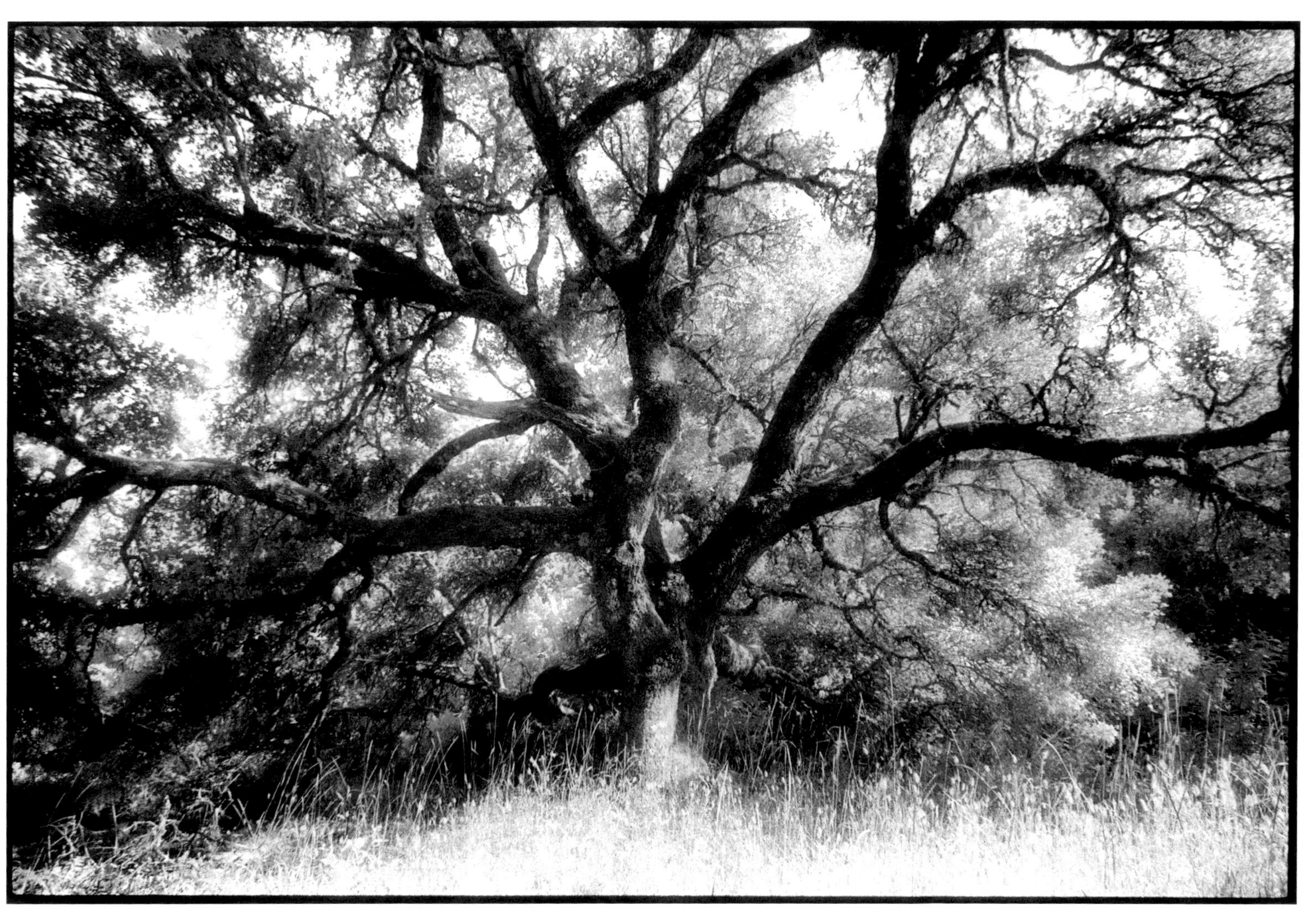

Plate 32
Secrets

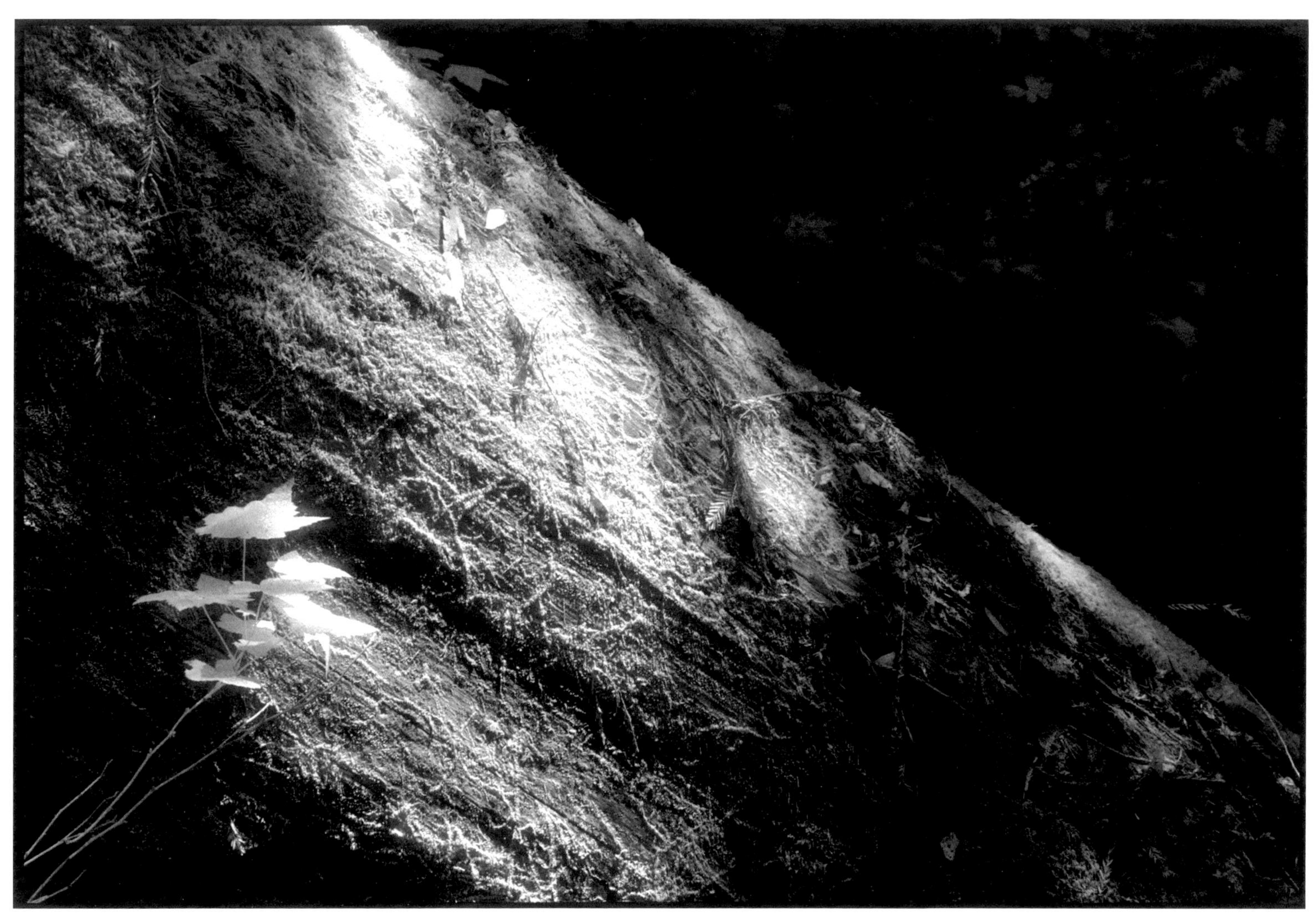

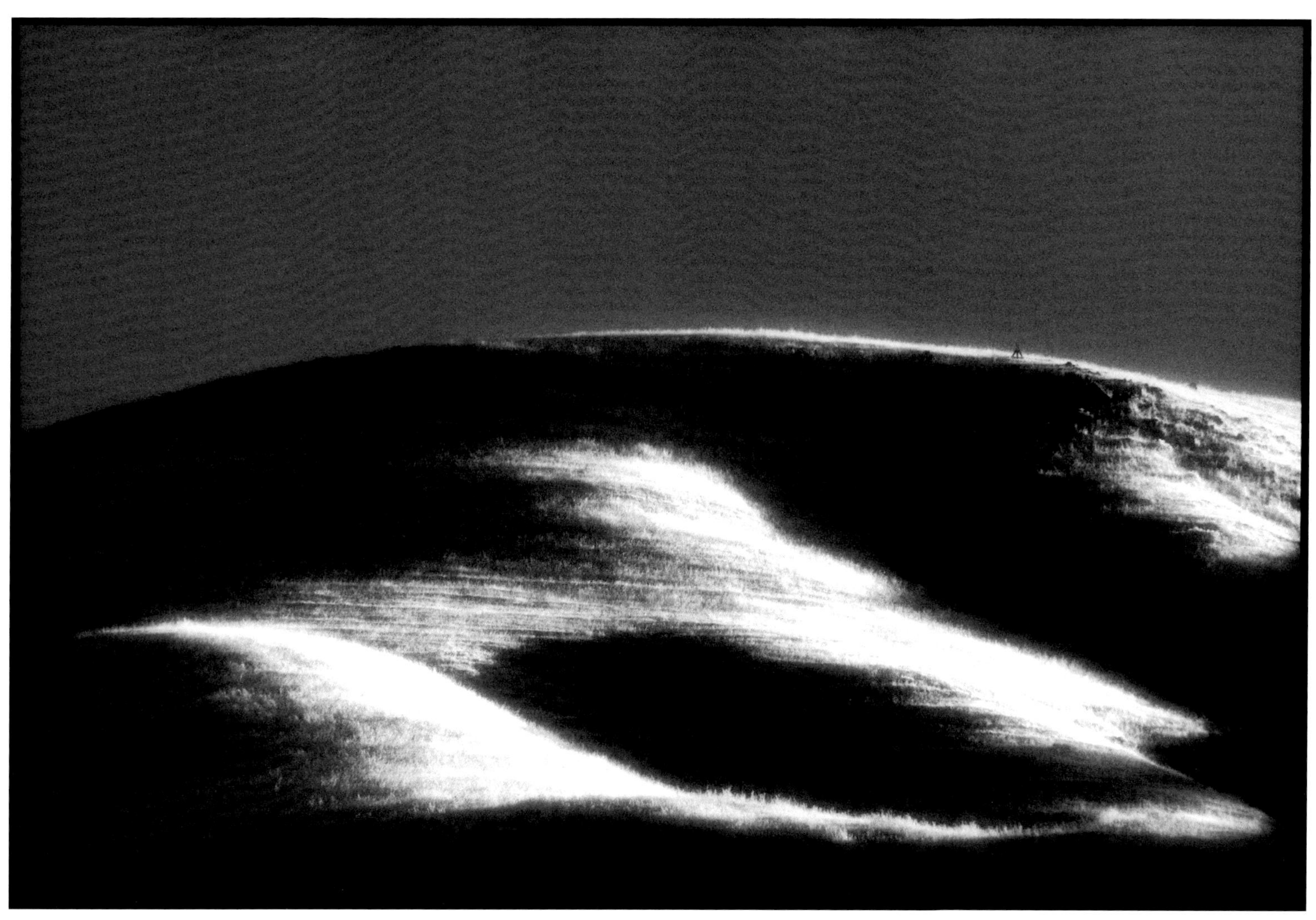

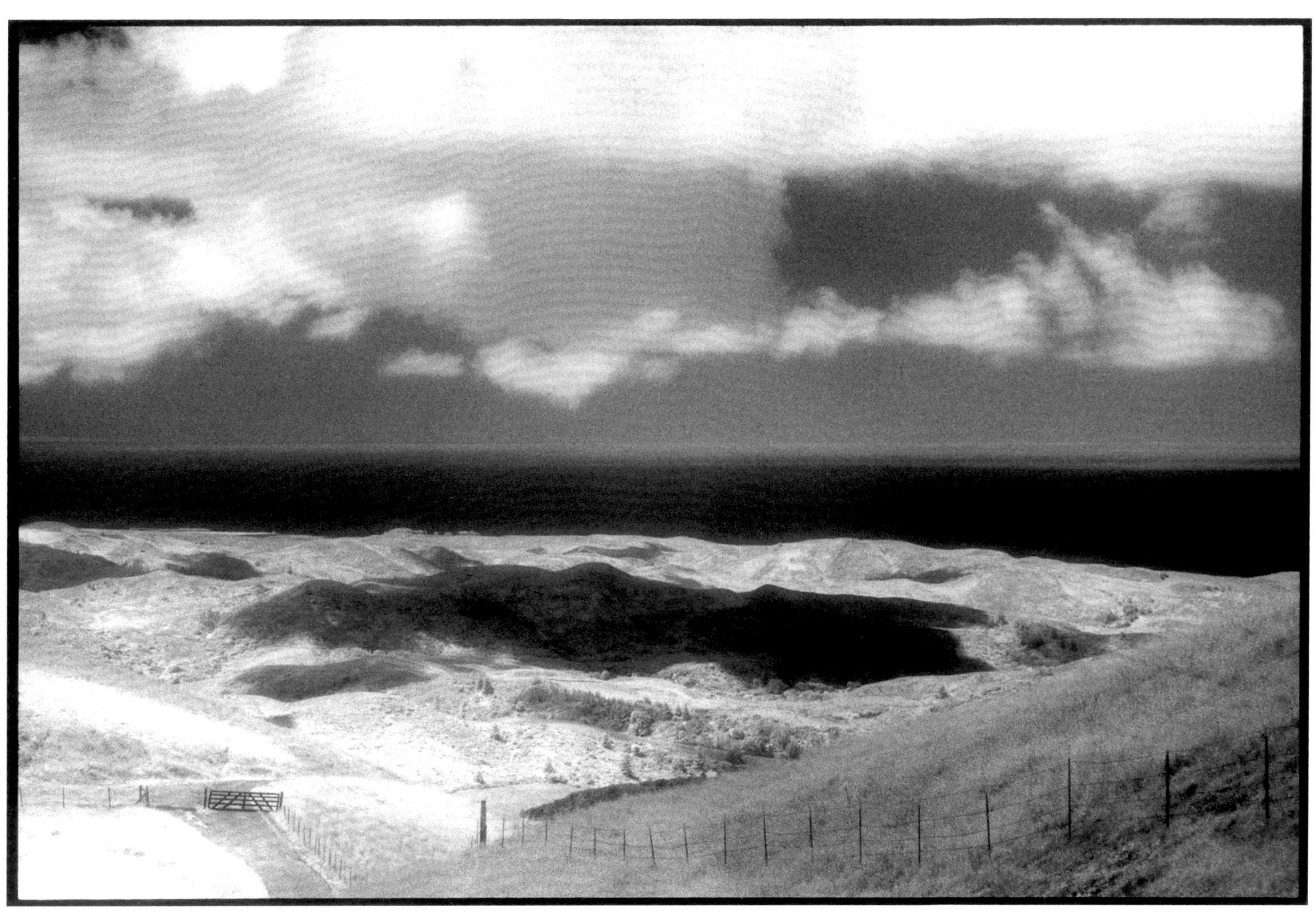

PLATE 35
LAST LIGHT

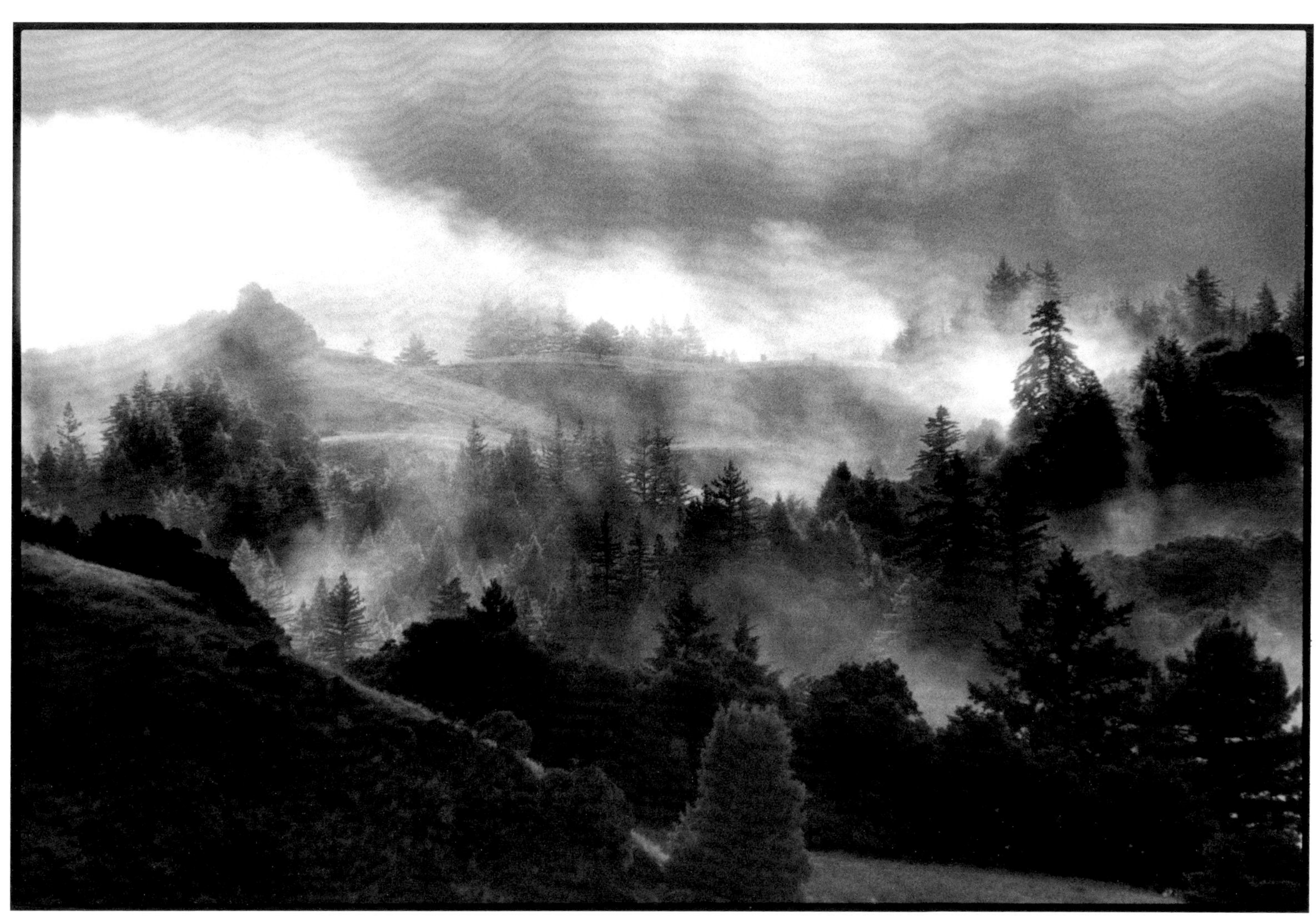

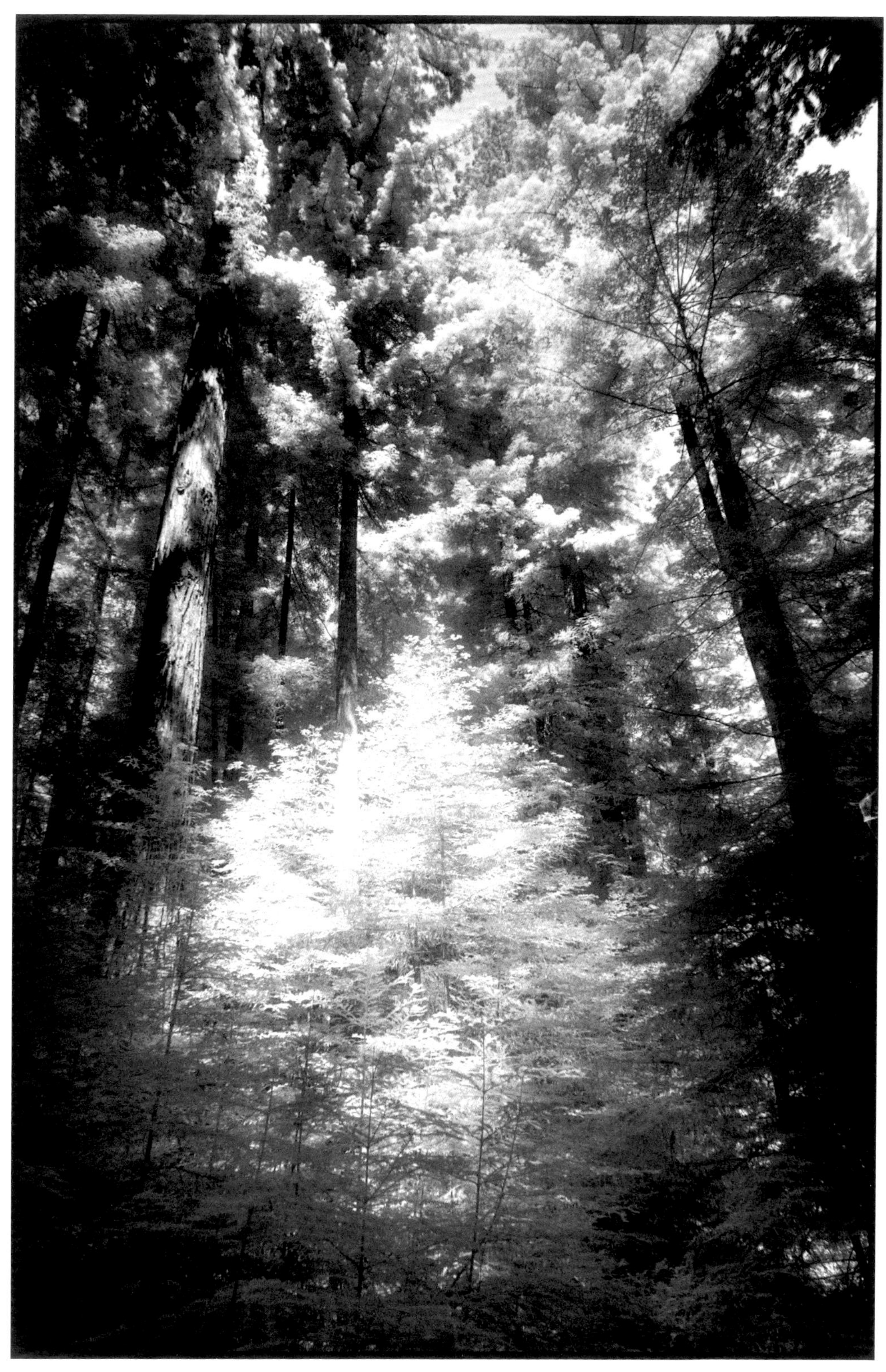

Plate 38
Constellation

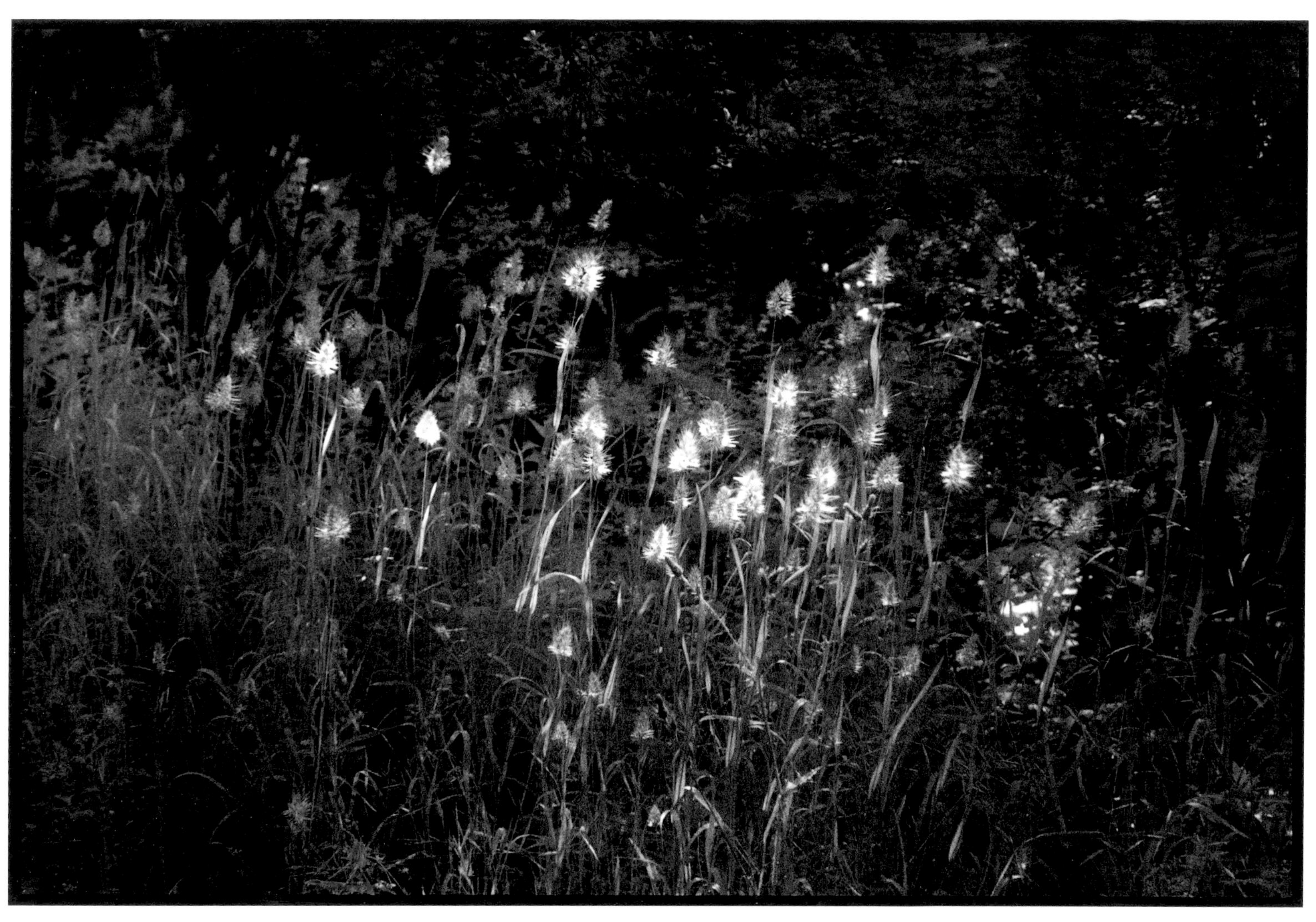

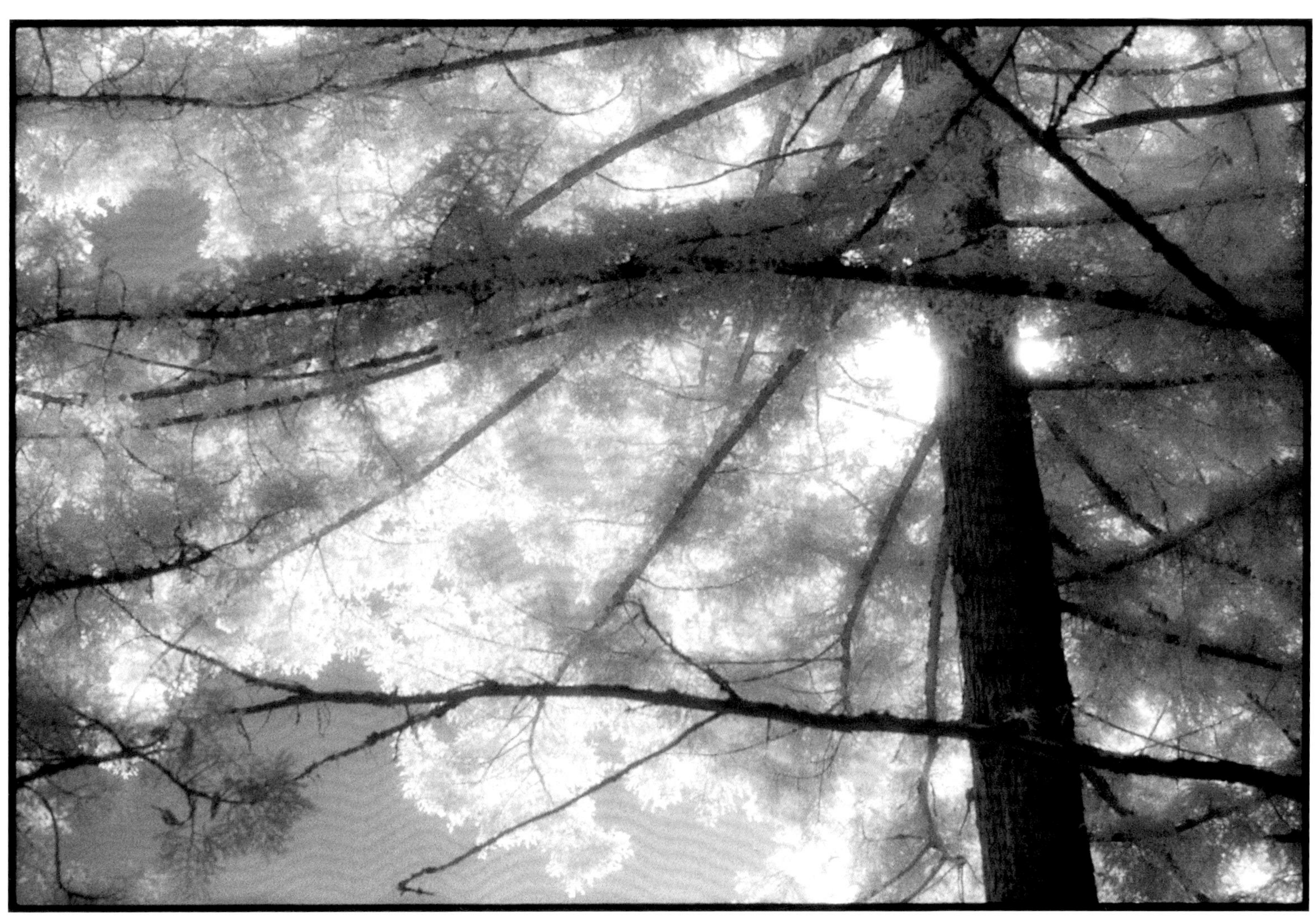

The land speaks to me in a voice I cannot always hear.

*Sometimes it is a dark and sullen voice, other times
it is bright, joyful and full of promise.*

Occasionally I am deaf to its language altogether.

*I work in my life as I do in my art to be a "listening"
for that voice, to learn what it might teach me, and to
share its truth with others.*

*—Robert Buelteman from the
Djerassi Resident Artists Program's Sunday Salon Series, March 1998*

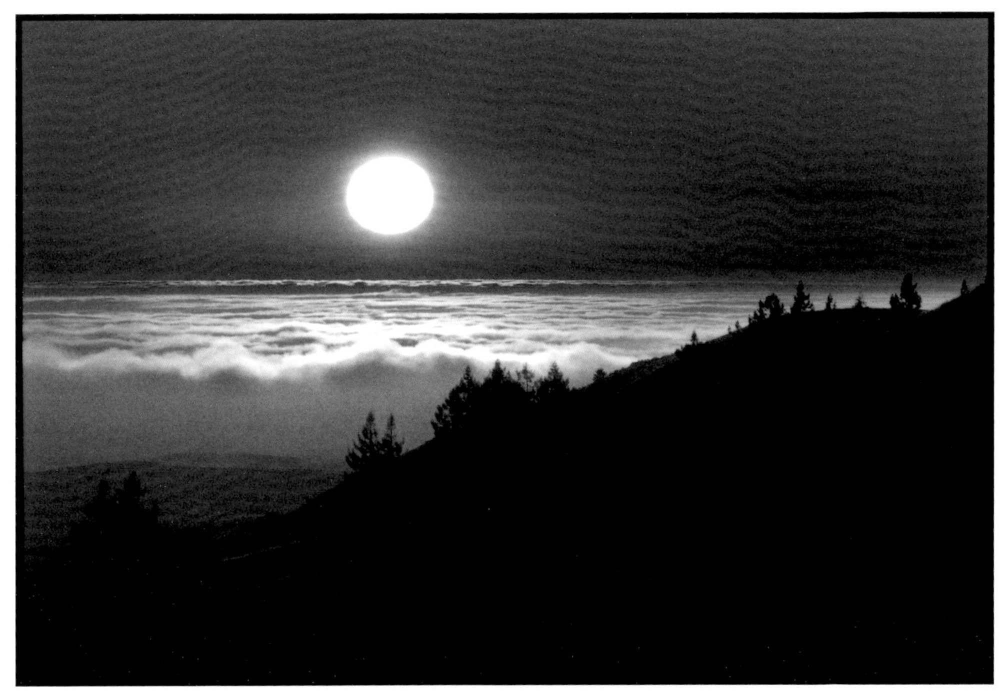

P late 40
D jerassi S undown

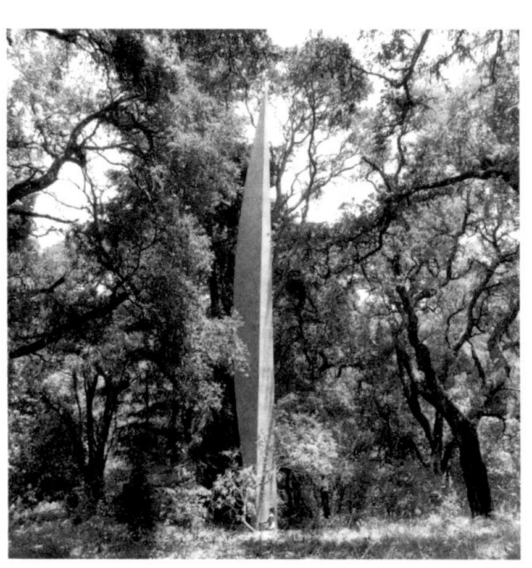

Cover/Page 1:   Tori Stargate (1995)

INSET PHOTOS

Page 6:   *Hai*/Andreas Straub (1995)

Page 8:   [Happening]/Susanne Cockrell

Page 16:   *Vanishing Ship*/John Roloff (1995)

Page 21:   Here

Page 96:   Untitled/Mauro Staccioli

Page 98:   *Not Here*/Seyed Alavi

THE PORTFOLIO

Plate 1:   Bare Hill and Clouds

Plate 2:   Untitled/Mauro Staccioli

Plate 3:   Barn Meadow

Plate 4:   Untitled/Seyed Alavi

Plate 5:   Sanctuary

Plate 6:   Cascade, Harrington Creek

Plate 7:   Coastal Hills

Plate 8:   *Wake*/Patricia Leighton

Plate 9:   Gridwood

Plate 10:   Grace

Plate 11:   Witness

Plate 12:   Snag

Plate 13:   Allen Lookout

Plate 14:   *Mona Lisa's Grave*/Mark Oliver

Plate 15:   Forest Grotto

Plate 16:   Source

Plate 17:   Djerassi Day's End

Plate 18:   Passages

Plate 19:   Ferndance

Plate 20:   Redwood Morning

Plate 21:   Trail

Plate 22:   Oak Afternoon

Plate 23:   *Double L Excentric Gyratory*/George Rickey

Plate 24:   Carl's Canyon

Plate 25:   Sequoia Sempervirens

Plate 26:   Mountain Fog

Plate 27:   *Sylvan Steps*/David Nash

Plate 28:   Father

Plate 29:   *Tori*/Bruce Johnson

Plate 30:   Redwood Meadow

Plate 31:   Reaching Oak

Plate 32:   Secrets

Plate 33:   Writer's Hill

Plate 34:   Horizon and Shadow

Plate 35:   Last Light

Plate 36:   Skyline Ridge

Plate 37:   Womb

Plate 38:   Constellation

Plate 39:   Promise

Plate 40:   Djerassi Sundown

All photos were made in June 1996, except those dated 1995, which were commissioned by the Peninsula Open Space Trust.

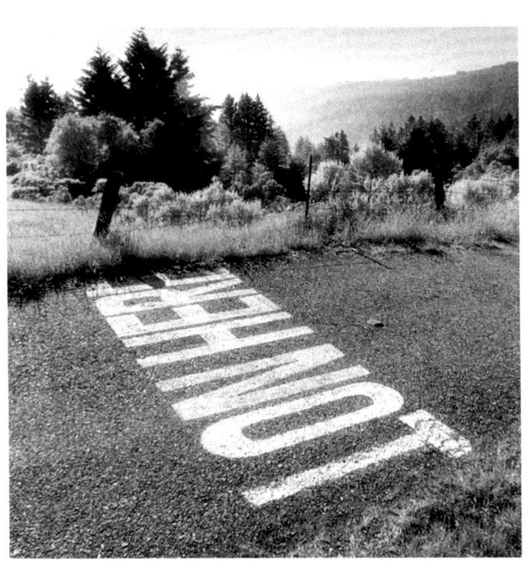
LONGER

Djerassi Resident Artists Program
2325 Bear Gulch Road
Woodside, California 94062-4405
Phone: (650) 747-1250
Fax: (650) 747-0105
E-mail: drap@djerassi.org
Web: www.djerassi.org

Robert Buelteman
Post Office Box 371239 / 848 Drake Street
Montara, California 94037-1239
Phone: (650) 728-1010
Fax: (650) 728-7540
E-mail: info@buelteman.com
Web: www.buelteman.com

Eighteen Days in June was printed in an edition of 3000 copies. These pages have been typeset in Mrs. Eaves Roman and Petite Caps by Emigre. The book was designed by 1185 Design, Palo Alto, California, and printed in Italy under the supervision of Custom & Limited Editions, San Francisco, California.